The middle years of this century marked a particularly intense time of crisis and change in European society. During this period (1930-1950), a broad intellectual and spiritual movement arose within the European Catholic community, largely in response to the secularism that lay at the core of the crisis. The movement drew inspiration from earlier theologians and philosophers such as Möhler, Newman, Gardeil, Rousselot, and Blondel, as well as from men of letters like Charles Péguy and Paul Claudel.

The group of academic theologians included in the movement extended into Belgium and Germany, in the work of men like Emile Mersch, Dom Odo Casel, Romano Guardini, and Karl Adam. But above all the theological activity during this period centered in France. Led principally by the Jesuits at Fourviére and the Dominicans at Le Saulchoir, the French revival included many of the greatest names in twentieth-century Catholic thought: Henri de Lubac, Jean Daniélou, Yves Congar, Marie-Dominique Chenu, Louis Bouyer, and, in association, Hans Urs von Balthasar.

It is not true — as subsequent folklore has it — that those theologians represented any sort of self-conscious "school": indeed, the differences among them, for example, between Fourviére and Soulchoir, were important. At the same time, most of them were united in the double conviction that theology had to speak to the present situation, and that the condition for doing so faithfully lay in a recovery of the Church's past. In other words, they saw clearly that the first step in what later came to be known as *aggiornamento* had to be *ressourcement* — a rediscovery of the riches of the whole of the Church's two-thousand-year tradition. According to de Lubac, for example, all of his own works as well as the entire *Sources chrétiennes* collection are based on the presupposition that "the renewal of Christian vitality is linked at least partially to a renewed exploration of the periods and of the works where the Christian tradition is expressed with particular intensity."

In sum, for the *ressourcement* theologians theology involved a "return to the sources" of Christian faith, for the purpose of drawing out the meaning and significance of these sources for the critical questions of our time. What these theologians sought was a spiritual and intellectual communion with Christianity in its most vital moments as transmitted to us in its classic texts, a communion which would nourish, invigorate, and rejuvenate twentieth-century Catholicism.

The *ressourcement* movement bore great fruit in the documents of the Second Vatican Council and has deeply influenced the work of Pope John Paul II and Cardinal Joseph Ratzinger, Prefect of the Sacred Congregation of the Doctrine of the Faith.

The present series is rooted in this twentieth-century renewal of theology, above all as the renewal is carried in the spirit of de Lubac and von Balthasar. In keeping with that spirit, the series understands *ressourcement* as revitalization: a return to the sources, for the purpose of developing a theology that will truly meet the challenges of our time. Some of the features of the series, then, will be:

- a return to classical (patristic-mediaeval) sources;
- a renewed interpretation of St. Thomas;
- a dialogue with the major movements and thinkers of the twentieth century, with particular attention to problems associated with the Enlightenment, modernity, liberalism.

The series will publish out-of-print or as yet untranslated studies by earlier authors associated with the *ressourcement* movement. The series also plans to publish works by contemporary authors sharing in the aim and spirit of this earlier movement. This will include interpretations of de Lubac and von Balthasar and, more generally, any works in theology, philosophy, history, literature, and the arts which give renewed expression to an authentic Catholic sensibility.

The editor of the Ressourcement series, David L. Schindler, is Gagnon Professor of Fundamental Theology at the John Paul II Institute in Washington, D.C., and editor of the North American edition of *Communio: International Catholic Review,* a federation of journals in thirteen countries founded in Europe in 1972 by Hans Urs von Balthasar, Jean Daniélou, Henri de Lubac, Joseph Ratzinger, and others.

The knowledge that Christ died for us, and other knowledge akin to this, move one to love — unless, that is, a man is an obstinate sinner — in an entirely different way than a proposition of geometry.

BONAVENTURE

There is in the time of the Church no historically influential theology which is not itself a reflection of the glory of God; only beautiful theology, that is, only theology which, grasped by the glory of God, is able itself to transmit its rays, has the chance of making any impact in human history by conviction and transformation.

HANS URS von BALTHASAR

God acts like a master who is certain of his servant. He counts on him today, because he already counted on him yesterday. It matters little to him if the servant failed yesterday or if his yes was hesitant or even inaudible. God hired him just the same. He is responsible for the Infinite which encompasses every call and every response.

ADRIENNE von SPEYR

Hans Urs von Balthasar

A Theological Style

ANGELO SCOLA

William B. Eerdmans Publishing Company
Grand Rapids, Michigan

Originally published as *Hans Urs von Balthasar: Uno stile teologico*
© 1991 Editoriale Jaca Book SpA, Milan

English translation © 1995 Wm. B. Eerdmans Publishing Co.
255 Jefferson Ave. S.E., Grand Rapids, Michigan 49503

Printed in the United States of America

00 99 98 97 96 95   7 6 5 4 3 2 1

Library of Congress Cataloging-in-Publication Data

Scola, Angelo.
[Hans Urs von Balthasar English]
Hans Urs von Balthasar : a theological style / Angelo Scola.
p.   cm. — (Ressourcement)
Includes bibliographical references.
ISBN 0-8028-0894-8 (alk. paper)
1. Balthasar, Hans Urs von, 1905-   . I. Title.   II. Series.
III. Series: Ressourcement (Grand Rapids, Mich.)
BX4705.B163S3613   1995
230'.2'092 — dc20   95-24161
CIP

Contents

Preface

The immediate occasion for this book was a suggestion made by the John Paul II Institute (for Studies on Marriage and the Family) in Washington. Father Benedict Ashley, O.P., the author of several works, including a large volume on the *Theologies of the Body,* was offering his students a course entitled "Contemporary Theological Paradigms." As visiting professor, I was invited to give a series of lectures on Balthasar within the framework of Fr. Ashley's course.

For several years I have been holding a seminar on Balthasar's Christology in the School of Theology at the Lateran University (Rome). In the seminar I examine several volumes of the Trilogy with the students. In addition, I have been referring to the work of the great Swiss theologian in my courses at the John Paul II Institute, also in the Lateran University, for quite some time. However, I had never attempted a synthetic reading, one, moreover, which would adopt the perspective suggested by the idea of theological paradigms. I was tempted by the proposal and finally agreed to give a few lessons in September 1990.

As summer approached I quickly found myself confronted with the proverbial question "What shall I do?", which did not fail to excite a certain amount of anxiety, all the more as the synthetic perspective of the course would not allow me such expedients as concentrating on this or that chapter of Balthasar's monumental work, thus using materials which I had already accumulated in my teaching. I was being compelled to risk a comprehensive treatment. But how could this be done in such a short time? Strickly speaking, even a cursory overview (an *Überblick,* as the Germans would say) was impossible. And then, did there not already exist for this purpose that slim volume which

Balthasar had intended as the *Epilogue* to his great Trilogy and in which he reviews in rhapsodic fashion its major themes?

It was then that I recalled the two marvelous volumes of *The Glory of the Lord,* which are dedicated respectively to ecclesiastical styles and to lay styles. However presumptuous it might seem, a title took shape in my mind: "Hans Urs von Balthasar: A Theological Style."

There immediately followed an internal dialogue regarding the impropriety of the word "style." I was supposed to say "form!" — and to allow that form which is the living heart of Balthasar's *opus* to unify my readings. My task was to discover the surest traces which they had produced in me so that I could distinguish the *principal* elements from the *secondary* and, above all, to find a path along which to guide my students to a first glimpse of the form of Balthasar's theology.

This form resides at the heart of Balthasar's total figure, of his Christian existence, of his singular call to accompany Adrienne von Speyr, of his works, and of his writings. And it resides there (as he himself taught, using Bonaventure's terminology) primarily as the expression of the impression which the glory of God, that is, Jesus Christ, the glorious Crucified, etched into his flesh in the course of his eighty-three years of life, sixty-five of which saw him take pen in hand to produce an immense harvest of writings, with the detachment of one who considers writing an occupation *faute de mieux* for a priest. His vocation, as he would say in an address to Pope John Paul II, was to spend himself for the Church. It was for her sake that he had been taken into service by a lightning-like call in a grove of the Black Forest.

To be sure, the stylistic means at Balthasar's disposal and, even more, his scientific and experiential knowledge of the things of God and of man were immense. "Perhaps the most learned man of our century" was how Cardinal de Lubac described him. For direct confirmation of this description, it suffices to stumble upon one of the endless number of reconstructions of the history of doctrine which are scattered without any display of pedantry everywhere in the Trilogy. In nourishing the reader they are second only to Balthasar's continual appeal to Scripture on which he mediated incessantly as the source of his theological activity, using all *four senses* restored to their rights by his friend de Lubac. Perhaps this is why we perceive that his writing comes so smoothly even though he refused to evade the labor of "scholarly" discussion, which was all the more rigorous in that the path he followed was original.

But this is not the place to pursue the matter.

There remains one more thing to say — and it is not so much that after my course in Washington I decided to rework my whole presentation and to publish this book. More important is to make the reader aware of what he should *not* look for in it. I have already stated that it is not exactly an *Überblick,* even though in many respects it furnishes materials for one. This is a good reason to consider it an introduction to Balthasar's writings.

Nor does this book undertake a detailed critical examination of Balthasar's philosophical and theological theses. These theses are illustrated, not debated. Given the endless number of pages which Balthasar penned, work in this area can be furthered only by monographic research devoted to specific topics, and this is the special province of doctoral and other dissertations in theology and — why not? — in philosophy, and perhaps even in literature. For this reason, the reader will not find references to any of the scholarly monographs dedicated to Balthasar, which are multiplying thickly and are often of great value.

What does this leave? Only that which I have understood, loved, and enjoyed in knowing Balthasar and in reading his writings. Only this, but arranged according to a form which I hope to have grasped to the extent that I have been grasped by it. Thus, in attempting to define Balthasar's theological (better: ecclesial) style (form) as I have experienced it, I hope to impel the reader to a direct perusal of his writings.

Such, then, is the nature of this book: an invitation to reading!

Rome, 2 February 1991   Angelo Scola
On the Feast of the Presentation

Translators' Note

A word of explanation about the apparatus is in order. We have attempted to refer to English translations — where they existed and were available to us — of works cited by the author in Italian versions. In the cases where we felt unable to match with confidence Italian citations to their English equivalents we noted the English title but also cited the pages from the Italian edition. It is a pleasure to thank Bishop Scola for his suggestions and corrections to our text.

J.T.
A.C.T.

CHAPTER ONE

Style and Form

*L**e style c'est l'homme,* "the style is the man," was a favorite maxim of the renowned French psychoanalyst Jacques Lacan. Does this title indicate the way to understand the meaning of the title: *Hans Urs von Balthasar: A Theological Style?* Or, if we prefer, in what sense are we speaking of theological style?

Although this Lacanian aphorism suggests an important truth, it is safer to go back to what Balthasar himself, a champion and practitioner of theological aesthetics, says about style. After all, did he not write a double volume of *The Glory of the Lord* in order to present us twelve styles "of Christian theologies and world pictures of the highest rank, each of which, having been marked at its centre by the glory of God's revelation, has sought to give the impact of this glory a central place in its vision?"[1]

In this sense Balthasar's concept of style appears less anthropocentric and more articulated than Lacan's. Its point of reference, in the final analysis, is the *Gloria Dei,* which is the absolutely free and enchanting irradiation of the Lordship of God on being, on every being — a glory from which irradiates a beauty capable of enrapturing whoever perceives it. For Balthasar style is found at the confluence of the Thomistic categories of *species* (form) and of *splendor* (splendor). They are the constituent factors of the *pulchrum* which Thomas himself defines as *splendor veri.*[2]

1. *The Glory of the Lord: A Theological Aesthetics, vol. II: Studies in Theological Style: Clerical Styles,* trans. Andrew Louth, Francis McDonagh, and Brian McNeil, ed. John Riches (San Francisco and New York, 1984), p. 13.

2. *The Glory of the Lord: A Theological Aesthetics, vol. I: Seeing the Form,* trans. Erasmo

Strictly speaking, then, a style is only the expression *(expressio)* of the impression *(impressio)* — the terms to which Balthasar refers are Bonaventure's — which a form makes with its splendor on the beholder, who, in turn, is always in some way enraptured by it. Outside of this constituent nucleus, there is no beauty and, therefore, no style.

Theologically speaking, the form of the beautiful is the glory of God *(kabod, doxa)*, whose splendor seizes and enraptures. And the glory of God attains its zenith in Jesus Christ, in that imperishable form which joins God and man (the world) in the new and eternal covenant. And more than any other this form requires the capacity for vision which belongs to the simple eyes of faith *(oculata fides,* says St. Thomas). "The apostles were transported by what they saw, heard, and touched — by everything manifested in the *form;* John especially, but also the others, never tire of describing in ever new ways how Jesus' figure stands out in his encounters and conversations; how, as the contours of his uniqueness emerge, suddenly and in an indescribable manner the ray of the unconditional breaks through, casting a person down to adoration and transforming him into a believer and a follower."[3]

This outline of the essential points already allows us to understand that for Balthasar a discussion of style would be unthinkable if it were not a discussion of form *(Gestalt)*. We will return later to the crucial concept of form when we treat the central methodological coordinates of Balthasar's theology.[4] For now it suffices to say that a theology, independently of the aesthetic means of expression that it utilizes (styles), does not find its form until it is dominated, precisely in its formal object, by the glory of God, of which it becomes a manifestation. In order to be such a manifestation, a theology must itself appear as the *expressio* of the *impressio* made on the theologian by the very glory of God. In other words, outside of the theologian's free experi-

Leiva-Merikakis, ed. Joseph Fessio and John Riches (San Francisco and New York, 1982), pp. 18ff.

3. Ibid., p. 33.

4. John O'Donnell was therefore quite perceptive in entitling his sketch of Balthasar's theology, "Hans Urs von Balthasar: The Form of his Theology," *Communio: International Catholic Review* 16 (1989): 458-74. Even before 1965, Balthasar had already given the concept of revelation as form a first systematic exposition in "Christliche Kunst und Verkündigung," *Mysterium Salutis,* vol. I, ed. J. Feiner and M. Löhrer (Einsiedeln and Cologne, 1965), pp. 708-26.

ence of rapture (we should say — but not without a certain hesitation on account of the wear and tear suffered by the word — of asceticism), there is no chance that his theology will acquire a form and thus be a theology in the full sense of the term. The apex of the form is well beyond the worldly stylistic means of which the writer avails himself (which in no way implies that style is without influence!). It is also beyond the external form of the individual theologies, which depends on the diversity of accent with which the formal object of theology itself (the glory of God) is regarded. It is located in their interior form, inasmuch as theology itself is "an active-passive radiance of the divine glory from the form of revelation."[5] To be sure, this primary form is accessible only through external form and style, that is, through a systematics (theological logic), through the concepts, words, and images coined by the theologian; however, the theologian can never forget that through the secondary form he must really reach and communicate the primary or interior form.

Such a vision of things deals a mortal blow to any formalistic discussion that aims to oppose or separate form and content, since the content (form in the strong sense) never finds styles ready to hand, but only emerging styles which are gradually forged by this content in the formative process of a theology. The free expressive relationship between man and God through Jesus Christ, the God-Man, is always at work simultaneously in any theology which attains a form. The content, or interior form, is already of itself divine glory in its worldly manifestation; this glory shapes the external form and style, which, though subject to the laws of man's creative freedom, live fully only because supported by that content. There is, therefore, a total harmony between content and form. Thus "theology is on the one hand an obedient repetition of the expression of revelation imprinted on the believer, and on the other, a creative, childlike, free sharing in the bringing-to-expression in the Holy Spirit."[6]

The individual theology as an expression of the impression of the glory of God originates, therefore, within a free-obedient relationship, which is not at all left to caprice or chance, since the content is, concretely speaking, the form of revelation and this form finds a

---

5. *The Glory of the Lord,* II:28.

6. Ibid. Balthasar had already offered a profound treatment of the subject: "Revelation and the Beautiful," in *The Word Made Flesh* (San Francisco, 1989), pp. 95-126.

binding hermeneutic principle in the Magisterium of the Church. Only in this already furrowed track, a space which does not constrict freedom but rather gives it a foundation, do theological missions and charisms take life. They are bestowed upon the Church so that they might represent, from a particular point of view which may have been undervalued previously, the form of revelation, either in its totality, or in some essential aspect.

At this point we can understand why, ever since the publication of the now famous essay "Theology and Sanctity,"[7] the image of Balthasar the theologian has been forever set by the contrast "between 'sitting' and 'kneeling' theology."[8] "Being on one's knees" has nothing to do with demonstrations of piety intended to substitute for scholarly rigor, which can only come from the long and laborious practice of study and research, but rather with the posture of the theologian's heart, which is that of Paul on the road to Damascus: seized by the form of the glory and thrown to his knees in adoration.

On the basis of this conception of form *(Gestalt)*, Balthasar, in the second volume of his theological aesthetics, chooses to present the style (form) of twelve great Christian authors whom he calls "creators of styles": Irenaeus, Augustine, Dionysius, Anselm, and Bonaventure, among the ecclesiastical styles; Dante, John of the Cross, Pascal, Hamann, Solov'ev, Hopkins, and Péguy, among the lay styles. The purpose is to fill out historically the abstract theory of form developed in the first volume of *The Glory of the Lord,* and thus document that in the measure of its faith humanity has actually succeeded in contemplating in Christian revelation some lineaments of God's glory. The styles of these twelve writers, to whom Balthasar could add still others (but after Thomas no theologian),[9] are chosen not only because they are of the highest order, but also because of their historical efficacy. As revealers of glory they were able to cast their light over the centuries of Christian civilization, but they would never have been able, nor would anyone today for that matter,

---

7. *The Word Made Flesh* (San Francisco, 1989), pp. 181-209.

8. P. Henrici, "A Sketch of Balthasar's Life," *Communio,* p. 329.

9. *The Glory of the Lord,* II:15ff.; *My Work: In Retrospect* (San Francisco, 1993), p. 82, where Balthasar speaks of a certain arbitrariness in his choice, but confirms that after Thomas "there is no longer such a direct radiance; hence laymen and religious come to the fore," ibid. p. 83.

to exhaust the full form of glory as it shines in the God of Jesus Christ.

We can gather two important points in passing.

First, here and only here can pluralism in theology find an adequate basis. Theological pluralism is not an arbitrary choice which the theologian makes in function of his particular style. It is, rather, the consequence of the fact that the form *(Gloria Dei),* in giving itself, always remains a mystery. It can never be fully comprehended. Balthasar does not hesitate to speak (though only from this point of view) of a plurality of Christologies in the New Testament, a plurality which does not impair its capacity to communicate a clear unitary faith in the *christological factum.*[10]

The second point to be noted concerns a conviction very dear to Balthasar: "There is in the time of the Church no historically influential theology which is not itself a reflection of the glory of God; only beautiful theology, that is, only theology which, grasped by the glory of God, is able itself to transmit its rays, has the chance of making any impact in human history by conviction and transformation."[11]

Perhaps the way to investigate Balthasar's theological style has now become clearer.

To be sure, we cannot perceive this style if we limit ourselves to its most external wrapping, that is, to the extraordinarily rich and fascinating use of expressive means which confer a wholly singular originality to his way of doing theology. Balthasar moves outside the well-established canons of neo-scholasticism, for which he, a student and admirer of medieval thought, does not spare his barbs,[12] but also of contemporary postmanualistic theology, which he often reproaches for having forgotten *the form of him who has incarnated the grace of God* in order to lose itself in a fragmentation which obscures the irradiation of glory from the eyes of the faith.[13]

---

10. *Theo-Drama: Theological Dramatic Theory, vol. III: The Dramatis Personae: The Person in Christ,* trans. Graham Harrison (San Francisco, 1992), pp. 143-48. On the theme of theological pluralism, see also "Pluralität der Theologie," *Homo creatus est* (Einsiedeln, 1985), pp. 301-11.

11. *The Glory of the Lord,* II:13-14.

12. *My Work,* p. 89: "Later, in Munich, Peter Lippert became a consoler of the young man languishing in the desert of Neoscholasticism." But this severe judgment recurs often, even recently, from the pen of our Basel theologian. See *Test Everything: Hold Fast to What Is Good* (San Francisco, 1989).

13. Cf. *My Work.* Balthasar expands upon this critique, sometimes making use

Nor does Balthasar's theological style consist entirely of what he would call the external form and which we dub, much more vulgarly, the systematic arrangement of his theology. This expression is not intended in any way to enclose Balthasar's work within a system, a thing that he abhorred, conscious as he was of the impossibility of imprisoning the unseizable glory of God in an effort of human reflection. A theology, on the contrary, has to be open on all sides, like a fragment out of which glory itself can shine, if it so wishes. If we consider, for example, the great Trilogy, the expression "systematic arrangement" explains Balthasar's option of developing the *intellectus fidei* of revelation in the triple scansion of glory, drama, and logic, as well as his peculiar hierarchy of the contents of the faith. They are choices which go beyond stylistic means of expression and correspond to precise reasons, to a specific logic (a systematic arrangement!), which we shall have to examine in depth in what follows.

We can obtain an inkling of Balthasar's style only if we can penetrate to the heart of his theology, letting ourselves be enraptured in turn by the appearance within it of the form in the proper sense: Christ. He is that complete form of Christian existence which forged the mind and heart, the life and works of the great theologian from Basel. This is also true of his writings, their external form and their style (in the strict sense). Thus his theological person itself (this is how he loved to define the Christian in terms of mission)[14] now appears to us as an ecclesial mission at which it is worthwhile to drink; and we can also start from his writings.

It is difficult, indeed exceedingly so, to attempt a description of this theological style (form) because it involves, when we consider it properly, not only the man Balthasar (as Lacan would say), but also the man fascinated by and rapt into the glory of God, the man whose life and thought seek to be a fragment in which the beauty of the absolute form, the God of Jesus Christ, can shine for us. Consequently it will be impossible in our study of Balthasar's works to avoid meeting him; we will have to enter into communion with him through his writings. Is this not an exciting new presentation of the high road to

---

of harsh words, in *Who Is a Christian?* trans. John Cumming (Westminster, Md., 1968); *The Moment of Christian Witness,* trans. Richard Beckley (Glen Rock, N.J., 1969); *The Office of Peter and the Structure of the Church,* trans. Andrée Emery (San Francisco, 1986).

14. *Theo-Drama,* III:263ff.

learning, even more, to understanding being, in itself and in its every manifestation? We are reminded here of Balthasar's well-known description of approach to God by way of the I-Thou relation. It begins with the wondering gaze with which the baby perceives the smile on the loving countenance of its mother and learns that being, the whole of being, which is shining luminously for him on that face *(pulchrum)* is self-communicating love *(bonum),* and, in this self-communication, speaks and reveals itself *(verum)*. [15]

Balthasar, who learned the simplicity of the child at the school of the Fathers and under the often painful tutelage of Adrienne von Speyr,[16] now asks of us this attitude which will permit us to enter, at least for a moment or two, into the form of his theology.

Balthasar's writings are many and varied: they range from patristic studies to a commentary on the Farewell trio in Mozart's "Magic Flute"; from the lofty discussion on the Trinity to his commentary on Dürer's prints; from close dialectic with Hegel to reflections on the poetics of Claudel or of Reinhold Schneider. And one could add many similar examples. A form traverses his writings, conferring upon them a unity which prevents their dispersal. Nevertheless, from this form, as from a beating heart, there branches off an intricate number of arteries and veins which, in their turn, nourish with life-giving blood an incalculable number of capillaries. How are we to enter? Whence should we set out in our attempt to reach the goal assigned by our subject?

The path I have chosen was not dictated only by my studies of Balthasar's writings. First and foremost it is tied to the precious gift of his acquaintance and friendship. I hope to have glimpsed the form of his theology and to have succeeded in communicating something of it, thus arousing in the reader the desire to go directly to his books themselves.

It may be useful to anticipate briefly how I intend to proceed. After this introductory chapter, I shall make brief mention in Chapter 2 of Balthasar's life and works, mostly referring the reader to autobiographical studies by other writers. In Chapter 3 I shall attempt to

---

15. "Movement Toward God," in *Explorations in Theology, vol. III: Creator Spirit,* pp. 15-55.

16. *Convergences: To the Sources of Christian Mystery* (San Francisco, 1984); *Christen sind einfältig* (Einsiedeln, 1983).

present the underlying motifs of his thought, those that, so to speak, constitute its driving force. This will be followed by a synthetic presentation of the major methodological principles which give direction to his theological reflection: (1) aesthetics, dramatics, and logic in Chapter 4 and (2) Christocentrism in Chapter 5. We shall thereby reach the heart of Balthasar's theology, which consists, in my opinion, of (1) the life of the Triune God (Chapter 6) and (2) the event Jesus Christ (Chapter 7). In what follows I shall discuss briefly two significant implications: dramatic anthropology in Chapter 8 and moral action in Chapter 9. I shall close in Chapter 10 with a few concluding observations of a general nature.

CHAPTER TWO

"You Shall Be Taken into Service": The Meaning of a Life

When Balthasar was invited to speak about his vocation in 1961, he recounted with precision the moment in which he received his call. It occurred during an Ignatian retreat in the summer of 1927.

> Even today, thirty years later, I could trace my steps back to that remote path in the Black Forest, not too far from Basel, and rediscover the tree under which I was struck, as if by lightning . . . and what suddenly entered my mind then was neither theology, nor the priesthood. It was simply this: you do not have to choose anything, you have been called! You will not serve, you will be taken into service. You do not have to make plans of any sort, you are only a pebble in a mosaic prepared long before. All that I had to do was simply leave everything behind and follow, without making plans, without desires or particular intuitions. I had only to remain there to see how I could be useful.[1]

These words that mirror his faith — which always remained childlike in the Gospel sense[2] — perhaps contain the meaning of his

---

1. *Por qué me hice Sacerdote.* Enquesta dirigida por Jorge Ramón María Sans Vila (Salamanca, 1959); and in the French version, *Pourquoi je me suis fait Prêtre* (Tournai, 1961), p. 21.

2. "Childlike in the best sense," an expression found in P. Henrici, "A Sketch," p. 310. On the importance of this theme, which often recurs in Balthasar's writings, see "Kind und Tod," in the last volume of the *Skizzen zur Theologie: Homo creatus est,* pp. 165-91.

entire life and work, both of which were dominated by the profound conviction that Christian existence consists of letting oneself be disposed of with the most total *indiferencia,* as his beloved master Ignatius teaches, for the mission which alone makes of a spiritual subject a person, a *theological person,* as he was fond of saying.[3] Ignatian indifference does not in any way signify negative passivity, but rather the most absolute poverty of spirit, the disposing of one's self before the surprising grace of the encounter with one's vocation, like a proffered chalice or a handmaid taken into service.[4] And for Balthasar this mission could in no way be preconceived (a term which, as we shall see, will carry great weight in his Christology), but only received, and wholly so, in the footsteps of Christ, whom the Letter to the Hebrews, in a famous verse (which appears only once in the entire New Testament: *hapax legomenon*), defines simply as "the one sent" (*apostolos:* Heb. 3:1).

To heed the call all that was needed was to await what would be required. It is impossible to understand Balthasar and his unreserved availability for the extraordinary vocation of Adrienne von Speyr apart from this vocational conception of life, which he chose to sum up with the expression *Our Task.* This is the title of a book[5] written expressly for the first public symposium on the mission of Adrienne von Speyr, to which Balthasar's own was so closely connected that he himself wanted it to be considered inseparable.[6] But his willingness to be "filled," to be taken into service day after day, circumstance after circumstance, found marvelous expression in his relation to all. I shall limit myself to the small example of my own experience. Rarely, even after his two cataract operations, did he decline an invitation to come to Italy for a lecture, to

3. *Theo-Drama,* III:208-20, where an entire section is dedicated to the struggle for the theological concept of person.

4. This exquisitely Marian theme recurs in a famous work of Adrienne von Speyr, *Handmaid of the Lord,* trans. E. A. Nelson (San Francisco, 1985).

5. *Our Task: A Report and a Plan* (San Francisco, 1994).

6. *Our Task,* p. 13. Moreover, he had already written (*My Work,* p. 89): "It was Adrienne von Speyr who showed the way in which Ignatius is fulfilled by John and therewith laid the basis for most of what I have published since 1940. Her work and mine are neither psychologically nor philologically to be separated: two halves of a single whole, which has as its center a unique foundation." See the acts of the symposium on Adrienne von Speyr's ecclesial mission; H. U. von Balthasar, *La mission ecclésiale d'Adrienne von Speyr . . . actes du colloque romain, 27-29 septembre 1985,* ed. G. Chantraine and A. Scola (Paris, 1986).

write an article even for newspapers and weekly periodicals,[7] or to grant hours of his precious time to students and friends who wished to see him in Basel. Often at the insistence of friends, I would phone him to propose this or that project, always fearful, indeed, convinced that he would politely refuse. Instead, he always considered the proposal with a cheerful tone and, unless previous obligations prevented him, would unhesitatingly reply in the affirmative.

He was attentive to everything, even to details, and did not neglect the smallest particular, for he viewed things with that availability born of indifference which allowed itself to be filled by the present circumstance, the mysterious sign of our daily dialogue with God.

After what we have said about the form (style) of Balthasar's theology, the point of this brief allusion to the deeply rooted vocational purpose which propelled his entire existence should be easily grasped. His theology, in fact, cannot be studied independently of the concrete experience of his existence as vocation. It would resist the attempt. How, in fact, could we prescind from that twofold movement — at once aesthetic and ascetic — which characterized his peculiar way of being seized by the splendor of the form and of giving it expression? Now, we find this distinctive mode scattered on every page of his writings and in every corner of the works which he founded. And it is only from this indispensable angle of vision that we can gain access to the understanding of his writings.

It is truly impossible in Balthasar's case to separate this work of the theologian from the experience of the subject who produced it. Let us not be deceived by any false scholarly objectivity. Sanctity and theology cannot remain long in an extrinsic relation one to the other. "True theology, the theology of the Saints, with the central doctrines of revelation always in view, inquires, in a spirit of obedience and reverence, what processes of human thought, what modes of approach are best fitted to bring out the meaning of what has been revealed. That meaning does not involve teaching anything occult or obstruse, but bringing men and their whole existence, intellectual as well as spiritual, into closer relation with God."[8]

---

7. One can gather an idea of the substantial nature of his contributions to the weekly *Il sabato* and to the monthly *Trenta Giorni* from the volume which gathers all of his articles published in these periodicals: *"La realtà e la gloria"* (Rome, 1988).

8. "Theology and Sanctity," *The Word Made Flesh* (San Francisco, 1989), p. 196.

Balthasar never tired of restating the urgent necessity of a new unity between sanctity and theology, precisely because he perceived so clearly the weighty consequences of the split, not only in the pernicious dualisms which have long characterized the history of modern theology, but above all in the desiccation of the very contents of theology. The theology of the saints, which always goes to the heart of revelation, can suggest what kind of thought and what sort of method are apt to shed light on its meaning. For example, what hints might be offered to the theologian who ventures upon the great mystery of the Trinity by meditation upon the scene of the Annunciation? Is this scene not an important biblical revelation of the Trinity?

> There we see, in the three stages of dialogue with the angel, Mary (the believing Sion, and therefore the tape of the church) initiated into her own particular form of service: the Lord is with you, you shall bear a son (who will be called the Son of the Most High, and will rule the house of Jacob), the Holy Ghost will overshadow you (and behold, your cousin Elizabeth also. . .). Each successive revelation of the divine mystery is occasioned by a fresh demand on Mary and her assent to it: the Trinity emerges in the context of her obedience, her virginal state, and the New Testament contains no revelation of it that falls outside this context.[9]

No theology true to its name can be separated from the concrete experience of the faith which informs it. How, in fact, could it be the *expression of the impression of the glory of God* if it did not begin from that most personal experience of the modality in which "along with the ontic order that orients man and the form of revelation to one another, the grace of the Holy Spirit creates the faculty that can apprehend this form, the faculty that can relish it and find its joy in it, *that can understand it and sense its interior truth and rightness.*"[10]

For these reasons, I consider as careful and as detailed as possible an examination of Balthasar's life and works to be an essential component of any study of his theological style. In reality, this task has already been performed by Balthasar himself, who, providing an important confirmation of all that we are saying, felt the need as far back

9. Ibid., p. 197.
10. *The Glory of the Lord,* I:247.

as 1955 to offer his readers "A Short Guide to My Books,"[11] which he followed, at ten-year intervals, with "In Retrospect"[12] in 1965 and in 1975 with "Another Ten Years."[13] Balthasar's concern in these writings is certainly not so much to offer a bibliography of his works as it is to explain the underlying logic which informs his work.[14]

Finally, we must mention an extremely important resource: the recent complete biography of Balthasar compiled by Cornelia Capol.[15] This bibliography is a comprehensive listing of all of Balthasar's works: books, articles, pieces included in collective works, prefaces, postfaces, and reviews, as well as the numerous anthologies of classical and modern authors in both philosophy and theology assembled by Balthasar himself. It also includes the series which Balthasar had edited ever since his days as chaplain of students at the University of Basel. In fact, his work as an editor was a function of this apostolate, which, upon ordination as a Jesuit, he preferred to teaching at the Gregorian University in Rome. Some of his writings, but above all the series, anthologies, and translations of authors which Balthasar deemed to be of crucial importance, would be incomprehensible apart from his pastoral work with young people.[16] All translations into foreign languages are also accurately listed by Capol, who is now director of the community of St. John. The bibliography can be considered definitive because Balthasar stipulated that no manuscript or part of a manuscript of his should appear after his death. "Everything which is truly important I have published myself."[17]

Having referred to these works as an essential part of this study, I would like to make a few more remarks concerning existence as vocation (to be *taken into service*).

11. "A Short Guide to My Books," in *My Work*, pp. 17-45.

12. "In Retrospect," in *My Work*, pp. 47-91.

13. "Another Ten Years," in *My Work*, pp. 93-106.

14. To these autobiographical texts should now be added the contribution by Balthasar's cousin, Peter Henrici, a professor at the Gregorian University. The essay, published in full in the English version, represents a privileged monument to Balthasar's life and work. I am referring to "A Sketch of Balthasar's Life," cited above.

15. *Hans Urs von Balthasar: Bibliographie 1925-1990*. Neu bearbeitet und ergänzt von Cornelia Capol (Einsiedeln-Freiburg, 1990).

16. P. Henrici, "A Sketch of Balthasar's Life," pp. 315-20. At Basel, in 1941, Balthasar founded the "Studentische Schulungsgemeinschaft," literally an educational community of university students.

17. *Bibliographie*, p. 4.

One aspect in which Ignatian *indiferencia* emerges forcefully in Balthasar is the relative weight which he accorded to his writings. Since our attention will be directed especially to these, it seems to me absolutely necessary to make explicit a fact easily checked in the autobiographical essays just cited. Balthasar always considered his activity as a writer to be secondary and *faute de mieux*.

> At its center there is a completely different interest: the task of renewing the Church through the formation of new communities that unite the radical Christian life of conformity to the evangelical counsels of Jesus with existence in the midst of the world, whether by practicing secular professions or through the ministerial priesthood to give new life to living communities. All my activity as a writer is subordinated to this task; if authorship had to give way before the urgency of the task of which I have spoken, to me it would not seem as if anything had been lost; no, much would have been gained. This is fundamentally obvious to one who lives in service of the cause of Jesus, the cause that concretely is the Church.[18]

Once again it is the mission received which dominates the person in his every dimension and in his every enterprise and which gives him interior liberty even in relation to theological activity, which in Balthasar's case showed signs of genius both by its quantity and its quality. Indeed, so great was his genius that his friend and colleague Cardinal de Lubac did not hesitate to call him a "new Father of the Church"[19] and "perhaps the most learned man of our time."[20] The Christian's engagement in the world[21] thus escapes being narrowly focused on an abstract theologizing, something which was never of primary importance for the great saintly theologians whom Balthasar

18. *My Work,* p. 95.
19. "Père de l'Eglise égaré chez les Helvètes" (A Church Father lost among the Helvetians), see H. de Lubac, "Hommage à H. U. von Balthasar pour ses 70 ans," *Communio* (French ed.), I (1975): 89.
20. H. de Lubac, *Un témoin dans l'Eglise: Hans Urs von Balthasar, Paradoxe et Mystère de l'Eglise* (Paris, 1967), pp. 184, 186.
21. The theme is developed in detail in the volume dedicated to the movement "Communion and Liberation": *Engagement with God* (London, 1975), which includes a valuable piece by Luigi Giussani. From 1971 on, Balthasar maintained a considerable friendship with the movement founded in Italy by the Milanese priest Fr. Luigi Giussani.

loved. It would have seemed to him an act of *hubris* against the mysterious glory of God that manifests itself with regal splendor and does not suffer any form to be set up before it as already given, because it itself forges the forms in which to communicate itself. Balthasar's mission is identified rather with the energies which he poured out for the edification of the Church, especially for the Community of St. John, which he, jointly with Adrienne, considered his work *par excellence.*[22]

Balthasar's vocational *indiferencia* thus became a calm interior detachment from writing, which, paradoxically, precisely because of this detachment, yielded such an important and abundant harvest. Since he was so free from every consideration of results, he could produce so much fruit; because his ecclesial vocation held the center of his existence, like a precious pearl which he treasured above all things, his writings express a beauty capable of ravishing the hearts of his readers; because he sought sanctity above all else and did not disdain to put himself at its service — and how onerous it was![23] — his theological work succeeded in sounding the little-known abysses of the mystery. Faithful to the conviction that sanctity and theology had to be linked, he placed himself at Adrienne's service, which also allowed him to reap the benefit of her many extraordinary intuitions regarding certain mysteries of the faith. And he took upon himself the difficult task of verifying their worth in respect to the teaching of the Church and the great theological tradition. His doctrine of hell and of "universal hope" are well known, but even his theology of the paschal triduum, as well as certain far from secondary aspects of his Christology and Trinitarian theology, found more than one precise source of inspiration in Adrienne.

Here too, in his conception of theology as "the critical enthusiasm of the faith,"[24] Balthasar appears to us as a bright star in the firmament peopled by the great figures of the holy doctors whom he studied and admired so much. John Paul II's decision to name him Cardinal, to which he acquiesced only with hesitation, is in some sense a cor-

22. *Our Task,* pp. 13-20.

23. In April 1956 he wrote: "Since January I have already copied a thousand manuscript pages" (dictated by Adrienne, author's note). See P. Henrici, "A Sketch of Balthasar's Life," p. 329.

24. See Origen, *Contra Celsum,* VII:44.

roboration of this. Despite the Lord's mysterious design in calling Balthasar to himself on the eve of his accession to the cardinalate, "what the Pope intended to express by this mark of distinction, and of honor, remains valid: no longer only private individuals but the Church itself, in its official responsibility, tells us that he is right in what he teaches of the faith, that he points the way to the sources of living water."[25]

25. J. Ratzinger, "Homily at the Funeral Liturgy of Hans Urs von Balthasar," in *Hans Urs von Balthasar: His Life and Work,* ed. David L. Schindler (San Francisco, 1991), p. 295.

CHAPTER THREE

The Appearance of the Form: The Logic of Balthasar's Thought

A few weeks before his death, Balthasar had the opportunity to present an overview of his thought. This was in early May 1988 on the occasion of a conference sponsored by his Spanish publisher and his Iberian friends from *Communio* to introduce the publication of the first volumes of *The Glory of the Lord* in the Spanish language.

In five pages the great theologian from Basel laid out the rational structure underlying the movement of thought from which his whole work takes its impetus and unfolds.[1] To speak of "the logic of Balthasar's thought" implies something dynamic: the motive force or engine of his thought. In this sense, if the term were not so devalued in our language, we would have to speak of principles (causes).

Actually in these few pages we can admire the appearance of the form of Balthasar's theology. The author himself is aware of this fact and makes a kind of reference to it. When a man has "published many large books" and is not a novelist but a philosopher or a theologian, he becomes aware that people ask themselves where they should begin "to touch the heart of his thought, because one presupposes that such a heart exists."[2]

Such a text, "despite the danger . . . of being too abstract,"[3]

1. "Retrospective," in *My Work,* pp. 111-19. A more developed presentation of these reasons can be found in *Epilog* (Einsiedeln, 1987). This is the volume that, in a synthetic recapitulation of the major themes, concludes the great Trilogy.

2. *My Work,* p. 111.

3. Ibid. Nevertheless, Balthasar immediately adds the remedy: "It is necessary

undoubtedly represents the best and surest way to enter the Balthasarian corpus. Although not lacking a certain theoretical roughness, it constitutes the key to comprehending the architecture which supports the Trilogy: Aesthetics, Dramatics, and Logic.[4]

A critical analysis of this text can unveil the wealth of the Balthasarian form and, at the same time, it will open a path through the dense thicket of his writings. Balthasar's aim is to show how the distinctive element in his thought fits in with the ontological patrimony inherited from classical philosophy. Ontological language, with its constituent components — such as, above all, the problem of the *ontological difference,* as it is called by contemporary metaphysics, or of the *real distinction,* to adhere to the terminology of classical metaphysics — is seen as the modality, at once more synthetic and more rigorous, of restating the problem of the relationship between essence and being. This ontological basis will then be enlarged by means of a subsequent reflection on the transcendentals, on the one hand, and on the I-Thou relationship, on the other.

"He [man] exists as a limited being in a limited world, but his reason is open to the unlimited, to all of Being."[5] This consideration is of fundamental importance because, when rigorously thought through, it reveals the *enigmatic nature of man.* How else than with the word "enigma" can we define the fact that that man *is,* but *does not have in himself the foundation of his own being?*

---

to amplify what follows with my biographical works, on the one hand (on the Fathers of the Church, on Karl Barth, Buber, Bernanos, Guardini, Reinhold Schneider, and all the authors treated in the Trilogy), with the works on spirituality, on the other hand (such as those on contemplative prayer, on Christ, Mary, and the Church), and finally, with the numerous translations of the Fathers of the Church, of the theologians of the Middle Ages and of modern times." Ibid., pp. 111f.

4. Balthasar states very humbly that this brief text is an "outline for the reading of the Trilogy."

5. Ibid., p. 112. This is a key theme in Balthasar's thought, which, as such, recurs continually in his writings. However, it is developed fully and organically in *Theo-Drama: Theological Dramatic Theory, vol. II: The Dramatis Personae: Man in God,* trans. Graham Harrison (San Francisco, 1990), pp. 189-429; and in *Theologik, vol. I: Wahrheit der Welt* (Einsiedeln, 1985). The theme is treated still more directly in this second work, which has a markedly philosophical tenor (even though for Balthasar "thought is a function . . . of faith," see "Theology and Sanctity," *The Word Made Flesh,* pp. 195-96, where it is stated that "all true philosophy outside Christianity is at bottom theology," p. 195).

What is the source of this conclusion? The experience of man's finitude and contingence. I *am* but could also not be. I know that I am finite. Many of the things which exist could also not be. This is a primordially evident reality. In rigorously metaphysical terms, and after Heidegger's clarifications, one could say that it is evident existentially, that is, that it concerns the very constitutive structures of human existence; as such it differs from something evident "existentially," something, that is, which concerns human existence captured in one of the numberless contingent aspects or episodes which concretely call every man to decision (first of all between authenticity and inauthenticity).[6]

Balthasar thus furnishes a sort of proof, as he calls it, of this state of affairs. Strictly speaking it is not a question of proof, at least not in the sense of a demonstration. It is rather an *inference.* An inference is the property whereby an antecedent proposition demonstrates, by dint of its own truth, the truth of the consequent. In the propositions we are examining, from the antecedent *man is but also can not be* we infer as the consequent that *man is limited but is open to the limitless.*[7]

But if essences are limited while being is not, then there is a fissure in being, at the heart of being. St. Thomas has termed this fissure *real distinction,* an expression over which philosophers still spill rivers of ink. This fissure is the mainspring of every philosophy, and, for its part, every philosophy, when it poses the problem of being in this way, reveals itself to be religious and "theological" by nature.

The fact that man is limited (that he *is* and could also *not be*), that his essence possesses a limited modality of existence, which proceeds from being, which is infinite and embraces all in one, without "consuming it" (everything that exists, exists because being is and cannot not be),[8]

6. In this sense, for Heidegger there is an important difference between *existential* and *existentiell.* See especially *Being and Time,* par. 4 and 9.

7. See, for example, J. Maritain, *Elements de Philosophie, vol. II.I. Petite logique* (Paris, 1946), esp. pp. 188-89, 193, 321-23.

8. *Theo-Drama,* II:209. Here Balthasar, in analyzing the structure of finite freedom, affirms: "In this primal experience, while I can distinguish between my 'mode of being' *(modus subsistentiae, tropos tes hyparxeos)* and my grasp of (universal) being, I cannot separate them." In this same part of the book he observes once again: "We are concentrating on the fundamental paradox that both things are unveiled in my own presence-to-myself: namely, the absolute incommunicability of my own being (as 'I') and the unlimited communicability of being as such (which is not 'used up' by the fullness of all the worldly existence in which it subsists)," p. 208.

represents the root of the question concerning the meaning of self and of things. If man did not have this experience of limit and of openness to the unlimited, it would be impossible to ask: "Who am I?"; "Whence do I come?"; "What is my destiny?"; "What is the origin and goal of all that exists?" From this experience spring both the religious thought and the philosophical reflection of humanity.

What has been said confirms, among other things, that man's religious dimension is the high point of his rational nature. The religious sense[9] is not another *thing* (it) with respect to his rational nature; it is the moment in which reason pushes forward into mystery and questions itself about the ultimate meaning of reality and of its destiny.

This is the origin of man's religious dimension, which, as such, exists in every man, regardless of how he succeeds in replying to these questions which constitute his very self. Whether he replies by recognizing God as a person, or by speaking of an absolute but impersonal being, or even by idolatrously exchanging a limited being for God, man will not succeed in suppressing the religious sense which constitutively indwells his heart.

Let us return to the enigma: man is limited but is open to the unlimited. What are the principal solutions which man seeks to the enigma? "One can try to leave behind the division between Being and essence, between the infinite and the finite; one will then say that all Being is infinite and immutable (Parmenides) or that all is movement, rhythm between contraries, becoming (Heraclitus)."[10]

These are the two extremes. When man finds himself facing an enigmatic polarity, he is always tempted to simplify its structure. The most common way to achieve the objective becomes that of transform-

---

9. This is also the definition offered by John Paul II in certain Catecheses of the *Holy Year of Redemption* (12 and 19 October 1983), where, among other things, he emphasizes the religious sense as the apex of man's rational nature, thus returning to the theme of some of his interventions at the Council on the subject of religious freedom (*Acta Syn.*, vol. III, pars. II:531-32: "Oportet ut persona humana appareat in reali sublimitate suae naturae rationalis, religio autem ut culmen istius naturae"; see A. Scola, "Il compito della chiesa: Gli interventi di K. Wojtyla al Concilio Ecumenico Vaticano II," in *Avvenimento e Tradizione: Questioni di ecclesiologia* (Milan, 1989), pp. 137-58. On the theme of the religious sense, see L. Giussani's unsurpassed study *The Religious Sense,* trans. John Zucchi (San Francisco, 1990).

10. *My Work,* p. 112.

ing one pole into a simple variant of the other. Another obvious example is offered by the history of Western thought in regard to the anthropological structure of the I, which is a dual unity of body and soul. There are those who maintain that the body is the lowest level of the spirit's fall, and there are those who say that the spirit is an epiphenomenon of the body.

In the case of the ontological structure which we are examining, an analogous twofold possibility presents itself. Either becoming does not exist and everything that seems finite and contingent is in reality limitless and immutable, or else the exactly opposite hypothesis is true: everything is movement, everything is becoming. In the first instance the finite and the limited will become *nonbeing,* an illusion to be eliminated. This is the solution offered by Buddhist mysticism. To some extent, it is also the solution of Plotinus: "The truth is only attained in ecstasy where one touches the One, which is at the same time All and Nothing (relative to all the rest that only seems to exist)."[11] Thus, nonbeing, the contingent, does not exist; everything that exists is eternal, immutable; everything which is apparent being must be surpassed in the search for *the being that remains,* for the immutable. In this perspective mysticism is conceived and articulated as self-removal from appearance.

---

11. Ibid. In this regard, we should not forget that as a young man Balthasar was greatly fascinated by Plotinus: *Test Everything: Hold Fast to What Is Good* (San Francisco, 1989), p. 10. See the outcome of this in *The Glory of the Lord, vol. IV: The Realm of Metaphysics in Antiquity* (San Francisco, 1989), pp. 280-313. In regard to the specific theme being discussed here, the following statement about the Plotinian conception of the radical fall of the individual soul, which requires asceticism as annulment in the universal soul is most illuminating:

> But when the individual soul within the Soul of all (which in turn gives form to the material totality of the world) is in its right place, in a state of well-being, it still has a tendency to separateness and encapsulation in itself. The world-Soul sovereignly forms its material embodiment in and around itself (so that this material element rests within the Soul that sustains it, like a net submerged in water), draws the fleshly order closer to itself and allows what is below it to come into its vicinity — we too "were there: all other men and even gods as well, pure souls and true intellect, united in and with the whole of being, portions of intellectual substance, nor divided or separated, no, but belonging to the All." But while all this is true at one level, we have now become beings tormented by desires, joys and sorrows, deluded by the phantoms of the material order and wearily sinking downward. (P. 285)

The case of Heraclitus is easier to settle because it is a case of pure self-contradiction. In fact, pure becoming, in pure finitude, can be conceived only by identifying opposites; but the identification of opposites (life is death; happiness is misfortune; wisdom is folly) makes it impossible even to mount an ontological discourse.

Balthasar does not go into theoretical detail in order to respond to the pre-Socratic attempt to resolve the enigma of the fissure in being. However, he does indicate the principal approach which Western thought historically devised for this purpose: the sensible terrestrial world is not the ideal divine world.

We are familiar with the articulation of the Platonic thesis: the pre-Socratics did not see the dignity of the relative becoming which is observable in experience, in the sphere of finite being (which for Plato is not properly being, but *doxa,* appearance!). There exists a form of becoming by which a *suppositum* passes from one stage to another, and what ceases to be in this passage is not the *suppositum* but *a qualitas accidentalis* of the *suppositum.* Plato, however, was far from understanding how becoming as such can be noncontradictory; but this would have required, in the final analysis, the inference of the existence of a creator God.

This is the great difficulty of pre-Christian thought: the inability to ground the coexistence of the infinite and the finite, the absolute and the contingent. In fact, being is absolute in that it cannot admit the existence of anything else; nothing can be other than this absolute being. Thus absolute being by its very nature is non-other (Nicholas of Cusa), because it contains in itself all the possible manifestations of being (the theme of Christian exemplarism).[12] How then do we explain the fact that alongside absolute being, which in itself does not tolerate the existence of anything other than itself, experience attests the otherness of the contingent? What need does absolute being have of the existence of the contingent? Only the concept of creation can furnish an explanation. Thus it may rightly be said that creation can be inferred from our experience, which attests to the existence of becoming.

In fact, becoming represents the nonbeing of being in contrast to the logos — reason — which represents the permanence of being (being is and cannot not be): thus becoming is contradictory! How can we justify the copresence of becoming, as manifested in experience,

12. Balthasar has dealt profoundly with this point in *Theo-Drama,* II:193ff.

with the permanence of the logos? It can, on one condition: that the becoming which we experience be brought into being by the absolute Being. And this is the inference of creation. There is no other possibility: the contingent is the outcome of a free choice of the absolute Being. This is the greatest demonstration (showing) of the existence of God, a more rigorous reelaboration of the five ways of St. Thomas.[13]

Balthasar is aware that this response was impossible before Christianity. Consequently, he alludes first to the outcome of the Platonic dualism of finite and infinite and then affirms the absolute gratuitousness of the answer given by divine revelation.

If the finite is not the infinite, where does this cleavage originate? Why are we not God? The first attempt at an answer is: "There must have been a fall, a decline, and the road to salvation can only be the return of the sensible finite to the intelligible infinite."[14] The second attempt can be formulated thus: "the infinite God had need of a finite world." Why? To perfect himself? To fulfill his potential? To have an object to love?

Both solutions lead to pantheism. In both cases, in fact, God, the Absolute, has once again become indigent, that is, finite. On the other hand, an urgent question poses itself: "But if God has no need of this the world — yet again, Why does the world exist?"[15] For Balthasar this is the most mysterious question touching the whole mystery of being.

Philosophically, or before Christianity, there is no answer to this dilemma, and the highest point attainable could only be the tantalizing question of revelation put to us in the celebrated passage of Plato's *Phaedo.*[16] This is the situation which Paul himself suggests to the Greeks in explaining how God created man so that he *might seek* the divine and *aspire* to attain it.

Creation is thus, strictly speaking, a mystery of the faith, a theological datum which in its formality can be inferred even philosophically once it has entered the hoizon of knowledge through revelation.

Balthasar's logic presses forward once the hypothesis of revelation

13. On this entire problem, see the celebrated article by G. Bontadini, "Per una filosofia neoclassica," in *La filosofia contemporanea in Italia: Invito al dialogo* (Asti-Roma, 1958).

14. *My Work,* p. 113.

15. Ibid., p. 113.

16. *Phaedo,* XXXV.

has been introduced: Will man be capable of understanding this revelation if God decides to reveal himself to him? Here we must answer,
on the one hand, that this God, who created the world and man,
knows his creature, and, on the other, that if he created languages he
will be capable of speaking and making himself comprehensible. "And
this posits a counterpart: To be able to hear and understand the
auto-revelation of God, man must in himself be a search for God, a
question posed to him."[17]

Human reason is created in openness to the infinite, and if it
maintains itself in this position (ontologically speaking it can never
lose it, but existentially it can do so in infinite ways!) it can understand
God speaking to it, if God decides to speak. Parenthetically, it is
appropriate to recall here that in theology we know not from below
(that is, philosophically) but from above that man is the question
corresponding to an answer which precedes him. And this answer is
Christ, the Alpha and the Omega, the first and the last, the beginning
and the end (cf. Rev. 21:6). For the moment, however, it is proper
that we remain with the principal ontological premise to which
Balthasar refers.

This premise, which in a certain sense is already familiar to us, is
the basis to which Balthasar attaches the *novum* that he calls his fundamental idea. In what does it consist?

Let us begin with a methodological preamble. The Greeks spoke of
metaphysics to indicate the act of going beyond physics, which encompassed the entire cosmos of which man was only a part. For Balthasar it
is necessary to speak of *meta-anthropology*. In fact, for modern man
physics is no longer of the Greek variety, but is the science of the material
world. And man is no longer part of the cosmos; rather, the cosmos
fulfills itself in man, who "at the same time sums up the world and
surpasses it."[18] Man, in fact, transcends the entire world at the very
moment when, in his capacity as microcosm, he synthesizes it in
himself. Man's spiritual nature, with its constitutive capacity for transcendence, thrusts him out beyond the world, and suggests an excess
with respect to the cosmos, while his corporal animated nature makes
him a living synthesis of the cosmos. Corresponding to all this, philosophy, more than metaphysics — a going beyond physics — must be a

---

17. *My Work,* p. 113.
18. Ibid., p. 114.

meta-anthropology which presuppoes not only the cosmological but also the anthropological sciences and goes beyond these latter in dealing with questions concerning both man's being and his essence.[19]

Here we see clearly Balthasar's theoretical innovation. The perspective of the entire analysis we have conducted thus far shifts depending on whether we continue to employ a metaphysical viewpoint, which regards man as a being among beings, as a part of the cosmos, or whether we adopt a meta-anthropological viewpoint. In such a horizon, the fact that man both synthesizes and transcends the cosmos means that ontological discourse takes as its starting point the existential analysis of man, that is, of his enigmatic structure (man is limited but is capable of the entirety of being), in order to go beyond it.

The theme of the real distinction, or ontological difference, is thus comprehended within a broader perspective, that of the existential structure of man, without losing any of its theoretical rigor. The consequences are not long in making themselves felt, because the approach to the same theme now acquires different dimensions, much more in tune with contemporary theoretical sensibilities.

Man is thus the point of departure of meta-anthropology; but if I pose the question of the ontological difference in terms of man I must first recognize that man exists only in dialogue with his fellow man. The horizon of infinite Being in its totality opens to him in dialogue. And in dialogue, correlatively, man gains self-awareness. This discovery proceeds according to the whole series of pivotal ontological moments. Let us follow closely Balthasar's description

---

19. The theme had already been placed, though in an indirect fashion, at the end of Balthasar's study of the complex historical fortunes of metaphysics, where he ringingly reaffirms its necessity even in its modern (meta-anthropological) acceptation:

> He [man] frees himself from this antithesis and so finds his true destiny (as master of nature) only by examining again the ground of this mastery, which certainly cannot be secured by unphilosophical theories of evolution . . . but only by a present act of elevation as ek-sistence within the Ontological Difference. In his consideration of the Difference, it becomes immediately clear to him that no possible evolution can surpass it nor even touch it, that no asymptotic approaches of the existent to Being are possible, and that thus no concept of human (individual or collective) wholeness can be constructed from the function of a mastery and domination of the world. (*The Glory of the Lord, vol. V: The Realm of Metaphysics in the Modern Age,* p. 653).

of the child's discovery of being which begins with the loving smile of its mother (it is obvious that this example is absolutely paradigmatic!).

> In that encounter, the horizon of all unlimited being opens itself for him, revealing four things to him: 1) that he is one in love with the mother, even in being other than his mother, therefore all Being is one; (2) that that love is good, therefore all Being is true; (3) that that love is true, therefore all Being is true; and (4) that that love evokes joy, therefore all Being is beautiful.[20]

The transcendentals are discovered in this encounter because in reality every encounter is an encounter with Being, and the transcendentals are properties of Being as such; they are coextensive with it and surpass the limits of the every essence. In the encounter with the other, it is not simply the other who reveals himself, but Being itself. On this basis, the whole perspective of classical metaphysics is placed within the new horizon of meta-anthropology. Moreover, Balthasar's position demonstrates a sound understanding which has an extremely valid psychological countercheck: in the security of this maternal embrace, the child truly moves forward into being, perceiving it as one, true, good, and beautiful. And if this primordial encounter, this original dialogical embrace is distorted, if for any reason the child's growth is imbalanced, it "misses" in some way the real, because it does not encounter being. Incidentally, Balthasar gives great weight to this thesis in Christology, when he takes up the very delicate question of the self-consciousness of Christ and states that he cannot agree that the I-Thou dialogue between the child Jesus and Mary is to be regarded as irrelevant to the constitution of Jesus' awareness of himself. The result would be to rob the incarnation itself of some of its reality, since a child who came to self-awareness without a Thou to address him would not be a human child.[21]

Balthasar notes that the epiphany of being is meaningful only if in the appearance we grasp the essence, the thing in itself, insofar as it reveals itself: the child does not simply perceive an appearance, but the mother in herself. This does not rule out the fact that we grasp

20. *My Work,* p. 114.
21. *Theo-Drama,* III:173-83.

the essence, as Thomas would say, only through its communication and not in itself.[22] This is a datum of great importance: if encounter is an encounter with the essence as such, then it is an encounter with a manifestation of being. Consequently, the more deeply I go into the dialogue with essences in which being subsists in a certain mode, the more I comprehend being, whereas the more I withdraw from these essences, the less I comprehend it. Here the idea of the concrete universal, which will culminate in the Balthasarian theme of Christ as concrete universal makes its appearance.[23]

The central place and, above all, the nature which the transcendentals enjoy in Balthasar's thought indicate how far removed this thought is from the Kantian-idealist concept of transcendental.[24] This is one of the differences that explains the serious divergence in opinion which, at a certain point in their lives, separated Rahner and Balthasar.[25] In effect, for Rahner, following Kant, the transcendental is, for all intents and purposes, never truly worked out thematically. In a certain sense, it can be said that for Rahner the movement toward being through the transcendental positively requires as its condition that little time be spent analyzing the transcendentals in contingent beings. The path is that of abstraction from the concrete in which being appears. For Balthasar, precisely the opposite is true: the more deeply I delve into the transcendental in the individual essences in which Being reveals itself, the more deeply do they reveal Being to me. The essence is a fragment in which Being subsists; it will never be able to deplete Being, but in this essence Being reveals itself and its transcendentals.

Just as being is predicable analogically, so are the transcendentals.

---

22. This point will be explained in detail in *Theologik,* vol. I.

23. The importance of the implication of the theme for moral theology is well known. "Nine Propositions on Christian Ethics," in *Principles of Christian Morality* (San Francisco, 1986), pp. 77-104.

24. The transcendentals "in Kant (in par. 12 of the analysis of concepts in the *Critique of Pure Reason*) are indeed an ancient but 'empty' idea, the truth of which lies in the formation of the categories of quantity, 'that is, of unity, plurality and universality as logical postulates and criteria of every knowledge of things,' which then in an ill-considered way are translated into 'properties of the things in themselves.' In Nietzsche not only are they turned against one another (truth is ugly . . .), but demonstrated as inwardly contradictory and thus dissolved." *Theologik,* vol. I (Einsiedeln, 1989), pp. XVf.

25. On this point, Henrici's essay appears to be too nuanced. See "A Sketch of Balthasar's Life," p. 344.

Balthasar's genius will show itself in the extraordinary elaboration of this principle. There is a difference between examining the transcendentals in contingent being and examining them in absolute being, in God. According to Balthasar analogy attains its full epiphanic density precisely in the analogy of the transcendentals; this is why the Trilogy is constructed on the basis of the transcendentals. The transcendentals, in fact, in surpassing the limits of every essence, reveal being, of which they are attributes.

Two conclusions, one positive, one negative, flow from what has been said.

First the positive: Man exists only through interhuman dialogue, that is, through language — the word. Why then deny the Word to Being itself? Revelation thus appears as a reasonable hypothesis, which finds confirmation in the great announcement of the Prologue of John's Gospel: "In the beginning was the Word, and the Word was with God, and the Word was God" (John 1:1). Thus God can reveal himself and does reveal himself by dint of the dialogic character of being. Man himself is dialogical. If man exists so much by interhuman dialogue that he discovers *who he is* only in dialogue, can we then deny to God the capacity to enter into dialogue with man? Such a denial would be absurd. We are justified in saying straightaway that, as Balthasar's conversations with Barth show, this dialogue is possible because of a precise Christocentric concepion of reality: man is dialogical precisely because created in Christ; it is not Adam who makes Christ possible, but vice versa.

Balthasar then moves on to the negative consequence. Let us suppose that God is really God, that is, that he is the totality of being which needs no created other and which cannot be anything's other; God will then be the very fullness of the One, of the Good, of the True, and of the Beautiful. Consequently, "the limited creature participates in the transcendentals only in a partial, fragmentary fashion."[26] Balthasar gives an example apropos of *the one*. In what does the unity of the finite world consist? Is it found in the species (every man is totally man) or in the individual (every man is indivisibly himself)?

Balthasar writes in a particularly illuminating way:

26. *My Work*, p. 115.

It thus becomes clear that the concept of unity, which everyone takes for granted as known and transparent, is after all just as mysterious as the other fundamental concepts of being. We do not know what unity truly is, we know unity only in the irreducible duality of the unity of the universal and the unity of the particular, without ever succeeding in identifying the two aspects. We shall never succeed in understanding unity beyond this duality. . . . We believe that we know what "a man," "a bird," or "a book" is, but as soon as we persist with the question, as soon as we ask ourselves if by this we mean "one" who happens to be under the unity of the species man or bird or book, where it does not matter which specimen of the species it is, or if by this "one" we mean this individual determinate being, who cannot be substituted by the entire totality of the fellow members of the species, then it is clear how much the unity of unity eludes us. . . . Similarly it is never possible by means of thought to close the break between essence and existence, or between essence and phenomenon, universality and singularity: every thought must recognize these breaches and must eternally circle around the mystery which they reveal. This mystery is not incomprehensible; it is charged with meaning, it is harmonious and satisfies every wish for unity. . . . We can certainly know of the two movements . . . but it is impossible to realize them both simultaneously. The existent in its revelation demonstrates its increasingly greater wealth and thereby its ineliminable mystery.[27]

In the finite realm, unity remains inevitably divided and polarized. This is true also for the good, for the true, and for the beautiful.

This conclusion is very important. It shows, in fact, the contingency of finite reality with its constituent law — polarity:

To interpret finite being it is necessary to have constant recourse to the phenomenon of polarity. Thus, the speculative schema of the metaphysical *composition* of different parts and elements is inadequate to describe in each case. Polarity signifies a rigorous intertwining of the poles of tension. And this could not be more evident in the polarity between essence and existence in finite being. The connection is so close that in its unity it constitutes the insoluble mystery of created being, so that every attempt to explain one of the two poles as the locus of the

27. *Theologik,* vol. I (Einsiedeln, 1985), pp. 173f. The theme is pursued further in ibid., pp. 169-73.

mystery in order to possess oneself of the other as the sphere of the obvious, is destined to fail.... Each of the two poles has in itself an aspect of graspability, but this aspect refers back beyond itself to the other aspect as to what has not been grasped.[28]

And the same law of polarity holds good, as we have seen, for the transcendentals in finite being.

To forget this great law means embarking, inexorably, on the road to idolatry.

Based on these premises Balthasar claims to have attempted by means of his writings to construct "a philosophy and a theology starting from an analogy, not of an abstract Being, but of Being as it is encountered concretely in its attributes (not categorical, but transcendental)."[29]

The transcendentals, since they are coextensive with Being — they traverse it entirely — are not juxtaposed but are implied in one another. Thus, that which is true must be also good, beautiful, and one. And this is so regardless of the transcendental.[30] The consequences of this are decisive on both the ethical and the aesthetic plane. This approach becomes a secure bulwark against any type of relativism and subjectivism: a thing which is not true can be neither beautiful nor good. But the same logical linkage works also for any of the transcendentals.[31]

We must not permit ourselves to miss the decisive significance of Balthasar's option for the transcendentals. In fact, his entire work, particularly insofar as it embodies an original methodology, depends on it. He decides not to take the analogy of being in itself as the axis

28. Ibid., p. 110.

29. *My Work,* pp. 115-16.

30. The point is adequately founded in several passages of the *Theologik*. See, for example, I:246-55: "Truth, goodness and beauty are to such a point transcendental properties of being that they can be understood only one within the other and one by means of the other. In their communion they furnish the proof of the inexhaustible depth and overflowing richness of being. They demonstrate that every thing is comprehensible and unveiled only because it is founded in a final mystery" (255).

31. Let us not forget that Balthasar has verified this conception (which, moreover, is a classical one) in the various fields of art: from music (Mozart), to painting (Dürer), to poetry (Claudel, Dante, etc.), to prose (Bernanos, Schneider, etc.). For specifics, see Capol's *Bibliographie* of Balthasar, equipped with a highly useful index of names.

for the construction of his philosophy and theology because he considers it abstract; rather, he opts for analogy in function of the transcendentals, inasmuch as they allow a concrete grasp in dealing with reality. The antithesis of the abstract and the concrete is made explicit by Balthasar himself!

Obviously this choice depends above all on the presuppositions which Balthasar has worked out already in justifiying the preference for a meta-anthropology over a metaphysics. It will be useful to recall once more that the second in no way eliminates the first, but rather comprehends it in a new perspective; nor does Balthasar intend to undervalue the classical approach permitted by the first choice — an approach that, incidentally, was never unaware of the *unum, verum,* and *bonum* as transcendentals, even though it allowed the *pulchrum* to fall into obscurity. He simply prefers this second path.

Wholly in line with the classical conception, however, is Balthasar's use of analogy as the sole instrument really suited to the construction not only of an *intellectus fidei* but also of a valid metaphysics. Balthasar strenuously defended and profoundly enriched the classic conception of analogy in his intense exchange with Barth[32] and in his friendship with Przywara.[33]

Having decided to use the analogy of the transcendentals, what is the objective starting point? Balthasar's approach is admirably summed up in three lines of the text which serves as the underlying pattern of the present chapter: "A being *appears,* it has an epiphany: in that it is beautiful and makes us marvel. In appearing it *gives* itself, it delivers itself to us: it is good. And in giving itself up, it *speaks* itself, it unveils itself: it is true (in itself, but in the other to which it reveals itself)."[34]

If we return to the I-Thou relationship, and to what we might call its paradigmatic instance (mother-infant), we can observe that the se-

---

32. *The Theology of Karl Barth: Exposition and Interpretation,* trans. Edward T. Oakes, S.J. (San Francisco, 1992), pp. 86-167.

33. We know that the unfinished dialogue between Przywara and Barth on the *analogia entis* was taken up by Balthasar himself. For Balthasar's several writings on Przywara (four scholarly articles, a contribution to a collective work, two prefaces to writings of Przywara published by the Johannes Verlag, and two reviews), see Capol's *Bibliographie,* p. 92.

34. *My Work,* p. 116.

quence which Balthasar lays out in the passage cited expresses the existential structure of the real just as he himself conceives it in his meta-anthropology. In reality, being, seen from the viewpoint of the analogy of the transcendentals, manifests itself most concretely according to this rhythm whose first beat is on epiphany. It is important to note that it is only by fusing the existential perspective of interpersonal relationship with that of the self-revelation of being in the sequence of transcendentals beginning with the *pulchrum,* that we can grasp the primordial structure of reality according to Balthasar's meta-anthropology, without needing to distinguish any further between subject and object. In fact, the child becomes conscious of its own being at the moment when it recognizes the being of the mother in all the concrete density of its transcendental properties.

When a man comes face to face with a beautiful being, he really does experience within himself a movement of abandonment and of attentive listening; it is as if he were hanging on this epiphany. For Balthasar the epiphany of being, that is, its beauty, is the true breach through which being penetrates into man and at the same time awakens him to consciousness of himself and of reality.

And since the transcendentals are mutually inclusive, the *bonum* necessarily follows the *pulchrum:* if the being which appears to me surprises me and captures me, if it satisfies me, this means that it gives itself, and if it gives itself this means that it is good. In this self-giving, being reveals itself as being at the very moment when it awakens the I to knowledge and to self-awareness — this is the *verum.*

If we place ourselves now at the beginning, at the beginning of everything, if we begin with that which is truly original, how can we not begin with the appearing of God, with his majestic beauty *(Aesthetics)?* But does not God appear in order to give himself? Does he not establish a covenant with man? Does he not put into play, in an authentic theodrama, his infinite freedom, intertwining it unreservedly with man's finite freedom, plunging himself all the way into depths of a mortal battle for the affirmation of the good *(Dramatics)?* Can God make himself comprehensible to man, rendering himself, the infinite Word, accessible in a finite logic and in finite words? Can this incomparable *pulchrum* which gives itself as the *bonum* communicate itself as *verum (Theologic)?*

We have thus uncovered the deepest movement of Balthasar's theology, thereby indicating the logic of his thought, that is, of his method in its fundamental structure. This movement is powerful enough not only to open the way for an original and complete attempt at an *intellectus fidei* of the Christian event (the Trilogy), but also, as befits truly original thought, makes plain the profound ontological implications of this event (which Balthasar sums up with the term meta-anthropological, which theological reason simply cannot do without. In this sense it is legitimate to speak of the appearance of a theological form, even though the inner Form par excellence is still implicit (but has already been announced).

We shall not, for the moment, attempt to follow Balthasar as he demonstrates how only Christianity, in the two fundamental dogmas of the Trinity and of the Incarnation, yields a response to the unresolved questions which flow from the fissure in being: Why does being exist, and not nothing? Why am I not God? Why did God create a world that, as God, he did not need?

To penetrate better the heart of the Christian event and of its principal consequences, we must first expand our knowledge of the methodological presuppositions of Balthasar's thought.

CHAPTER FOUR

The Bases of the
Theological Method
I. Aesthetics, Dramatics, Logic

Balthasar summarized in one word the ontological foundations of the exercise of theological reasoning, that is, of that function of reason within faith which develops theology as a science of faith: meta-anthropology. Theological reason has an absolute need of meta-anthropology in order to unfold with sufficient breadth of vision the entire *intellectus fidei* of revelation, that is, of the event of Christ. Otherwise it risks the fatal isolation in which "theology, rendered uncertain, is prone to cut off the branch on which it sits with an exegetical rationalism or to burst forth into politics."[1] Behind the neologism meta-anthropology, moreover, is the confluence of three ontological *demarches* skillfully fused into a unity: (1) the existential (in Heidegger's sense),[2] in which man's *Dasein* is grasped both in its

---

1. *Theologik,* vol. I (Einsiedeln, 1985), pp. xiv-xv.
2. Balthasar is well aware of the significance and of the limits of Heidegger's dialectic of existential/*existentiell,* as well as of the limits of the theme of the ontological difference. He is also well aware of the objective insufficiency of Heidegger's thought. In fact, he devoted a chapter to Heidegger in the third volume of *Apokalypse der deutschen Seele: Die Vergöttlichung des Todes* (Salzburg, 1939), and a chapter in *The Glory of the Lord, vol. VII: Theology: The New Covenant* (San Francisco, 1989). Thus, apropos of a point as delicate as the application of the ontological difference to Trinitarian theology, Balthasar writes:

> Martin Heidegger has criticized the concept of divine being as subsistent and has stigmatized the speculation on being inherited from the Greeks as "onto-

limitation and in its openness to the unlimited (Balthasar also frequently explores this point at its classically ontological foundation: the real distinction between essences and being); (2) the dialogical *demarche:* the I-Thou relation, the encounter analyzed in itself and, once again, in its ontological roots as the simultaneous opening of the space of the I and of the space of being (and thus of the thou- and we- dimensions);[3] (3) that of the analogy of the transcendentals between God and his creature, an analogy which does not ignore the analogy of being in itself as its foundation.[4]

The question now arises: What are the methodological principles which enable the transposition of the triple analogy of the beautiful, the good, and the true into the Trilogy of Aesthetics, Dramatics, and Logic? Moreover, how and on what grounds are the three panels of the triptych internally divided so as to give occasion to the fifteen volumes which compose it (not to mention the somewhat rhapsodic reprise entitled *Epilogue*)?[5]

It is appropriate to pause for a moment to consider the answer to this twofold query if we are to open a passage to the inner form of Balthasar's theology, the central mysteries of the Trinity and of the Incarnation.

Once again, a series of questions present themselves at the very threshold of such an undertaking. Why begin with aesthetics? Is this not, in a certain sense, a subversion of the objective order of the

----

theology," as a representation of the divine being projected according to the model of finite *Dasein* which exists in the ontological difference. The notion of ontological difference thus seems to him the strongest reason for the oblivion of being. . . . This *would concern* our exposition only if we conceived the Persons in God as essences to which the divine being would belong in the same way in which worldly existents are marked by the ontological difference. *There is absolutely no question of this in a Christian doctrine of truth. Theologik, vol. II: Wahrheit Gottes* (Einsiedeln, 1990), p. 125, n. 10. Balthasar has, moreover, carefully studied the problem of the *existentiell* in an important chapter of his *The Theology of Karl Barth,* pp. 220-24.

3. The subject is studied both in the *Theo-Drama,* II:207ff. and in the *Theologik,* I:80-128).

4. The problem is given a thoroughgoing treatment in *Theologik.*

5. Whoever might think that it contains a summary of the Trilogy would be disappointed. It consists, rather, of unsystematic reflections upon the principal subjects discussed: *Epilog,* p. 7.

transcendentals? Does not Balthasar himself affirm that the "foundational transcendental" is unity?[6] Is it not the case that historically speaking the beautiful is the last to appear in the sequence of the transcendentals and, what is more, that its status is still a matter of dispute? There is an even more radical question, though it too derives its force from the hierarchy of the transcendentals: Does not the collocation of aesthetics before logic and dramatics run counter to the articulation of a theological discourse which has any pretensions to saying something meaningful?[7] Balthasar mentions in this connection Rahner's objection based on the Trinitarian nature of revelation. If God the Father is the originating ground of the divinity, he reveals himself to us in only two divine hypostases: in the Son who reveals the truth of the Father and in the Spirit who manifests his love in us.

> This transcendental duality [of knowledge and of love] can no longer be integrated on the part of other determinations (for example, by an equally original "beautiful" . . .). This is so not only because otherwise a real knowledge of the only two intratrinitarian processions would be mortally threatened and the fundamental axiom of identity between the economic and the immanent Trinity could no longer be maintained. Rather, if will, liberty, *bonum* are understood in their true and full essence, as love for the person, which not only reaches out towards the person, but rests in the person's full goodness and splendor, then one cannot see any reason at all for adding a third power to this duality.[8]

Balthasar had already replied to this complex of questions from the theoretical point of view (meta-anthropology) in taking up the dialogical dimension to explain man's existential condition (or, more radically, the question of the ontological difference).

The dialogical dimension presents a distinctive phenomenological order according to which, first of all, a being appears, a form shines. It is thus that the transcendentals appear in an unfolding sequence in virtue of the principle of their mutual presentation. Balthasar does not so commit himself to a formal justification of this order as to claim that it represents the objective ontological hierarchy. This, in fact,

---

6. *Theologik,* I:vi.

7. Ibid., p. XIX.

8. Karl Rahner, "Der dreifaltige Gott als tranzendenter Urgrund der Heils-geschichte," in *Mysterium Salutis,* vol. II (1967), p. 378.

would require placing unity first, truth next, and beauty only at the end. Nevertheless, unity as a transcendental "will be able to be investigated only after we have treated thematically the other transcendentals,"[9] and, on the other hand, the principle of circumincession places no objection to beginning with the *pulchrum*.

If we pass next to the plane of theology, the decision to begin with Aesthetics, that is, under the sign of glory, in addition to respecting the generally valid sequence illustrated above, simply reproposes a fundamental theology.[10] In any case, what counts most is the awareness that "Today's positivist/atheist man, who has made himself blind not only to theology but even philosophy, should, once placed before the phenomenon of Christ (the splendor of the glorious and sublime God), once again learn 'to see.'"[11] As further confirmation Balthasar adds that whoever is struck by the splendor of Christ, and in him of the Triune God, is initiated into the required answer. Today more than ever, Christian *praxis* can essentially follow only from *theoria*.[12] The very logic of the revelation of God, which rightly puts a high premium on glory *(kabod, doxa),* offers another important proof of this, because "God does not come primarily as a teacher for us ('true'), as a useful 'redeemer' for us ('good'), but to display and to radiate himself, the splendor of his eternal triune love in that 'disinterestedness' that true love has in common with true beauty. For the glory of God the world was created through it and for its sake the world is also redeemed."[13] Even though the ascent to God through aesthetics may appear unusual, it alone can grasp the divine "without obscuring it beforehand by an instrumental relationship to the cosmos (which, imperfect, calls for divine completion) or to man (who, still more imperfect and lost in sin, requires a savior)."[14]

Rahner's objection will be answered fully in the sequences of Trinitarian theology which Balthasar will develop in the Aesthetics,[15]

9. *Theologik,* I:VIII. The subject is studied in detail at pp. 169-75.

10. Ibid., p. XX, where Balthasar speaks also of a similarity "with an earlier apologetic."

11. Ibid., p. XX.

12. Ibid., p. XXI.

13. *My Work,* p. 80.

14. Ibid., p. 81.

15. See *The Glory of the Lord, vol. VII: Theology: The New Covenant* (San Francisco, 1969).

as well as in the Dramatics[16] and the Logic.[17] Especially in the Logic, Balthasar will be led to justify the existence of the transcendentals in God and to study the relationship between the Trinity and the transcendentals.[18] If the latter are coextensive with being they also pertain to the supreme Being: "Now the transcendentals cannot be simply and exclusively attributed to the divine essence as such, because the *Imago,* and thus the exemplarity of every created thing, is a proper name of the Son, Liberality, and consequently the basis of why creation becomes real in principle, is a proper name of the Holy Spirit."[19] The reply to Rahner is implicit in this observation. And, in fact, by virtue of the existence of the transcendentals in God, Balthasar, in full harmony with the whole methodological principle governing the elaboration of his theology (analogy of the transcendentals!), explores the analogy between the Triune God and the creature in all its dimensions. Balthasar is constantly aware of the delicate nature of such a methodological approach: "We could ask ourselves if a similar treatment of the transcendentals (that in God co-penetrate the essence and characterize the Hypostases as such) attributes sufficient value to the *'maior dissimilitudo'* between God and the creature . . . however, a single glance at the necessary Trinity of the divine Being and at the contingency of the billions of individuals of humanity suffices to make this greater dissimilarity immediately obvious."[20]

Once again we glimpse how the disagreement between the two great theologians of the contemporary era rests precisely, as we noted in the previous chapter, on their different conceptions of the transcendentals. And we are dealing with a principle that makes all its weight felt in the principal theological treatises.

Let us move on now to the individual parts of the Trilogy. We

16. *Theo-Drama,* III: 83-91 (Trinitarian inversion); *Theo-Drama: Theological Dramatic Theory, vol. IV: The Action* (San Francisco, 1992), pp. 317-406, where an entire section is dedicated to the problem of the immanent and economic Trinity; *Theodramatik, vol. IV: Das Endspiel* (Einsiedeln, 1983): the whole volume has a Trinitarian thrust, even though it deals directly with eschatological problems.

17. *Theologik,* vol. II; see also pp. 99-150 of *Theologik, vol. III: Der Geist der Wahrheit* (Einsiedeln, 1987), which is entirely dedicated to the Holy Spirit.

18. *Theologik,* II:159-64.

19. Ibid., p. 161.

20. Ibid., p. 164.

know already that the idea of the splendor of the glory which strikes (the glory can thus be perceived) and enraptures dominates the perspective of the first panel of the triptych: this indicates, in formal terms, the movement which governs the whole of Balthasar's theological *Aesthetics*. This movement is concentrated in the decisive category of form — a form which functions as the load-bearing structure, supporting the seven volumes of the aesthetics. We have already spoken about form in the introduction. Here it will suffice to restate a sort of description cum definition. Form *(Gestalt)* is the densely concrete structure of being (an "inside" and an "outside" inseparably joined); it is a concrete dynamic figure which pervades every single being by unifying it in all its parts, and which opens it to that Being which really "informs" it, gives it form (whose expression it thus is), and renders it capable of giving off in turn its own splendor. Form, in the supreme sense, is thus the Triune God, whose mysterious splendor, whose glory, while remaining absolutely itself, traverses the entire boundless field of beings impressing its mark upon them *(impressio),* so that they in their turn may express *(expressio)* the beauty received.

Is man capable of perceiving the form? And can he, above all, distinguish the supreme form irradiated by the glory of God from the thousand other phenomena of this world? The first volume of *The Glory of the Lord, Seeing the Form* undertakes the task of answering these questions on the subjective plane of the experience of the faith and on the objective plane of the unveiling of the event of revelation, reaching the point of posing the conditions for grasping the form of the one who abased himself for us on the cross, finding there through the power of the Spirit the glory of the Father. To grasp this form, to make of it in some way an interior experience, man also possesses a pre-comprehension in his human structure.

Two volumes, *The Realm of Metaphysics in Antiquity* (vol. IV) and *The Realm of Metaphysics in the Modern Age* (vol. V), are dedicated to clarifying this pre-comprehension in an explicit manner.[17] These volumes follow the evolution of this capacity for pre-comprehension throughout history until reaching the anguished question which emerges from modern thought: "How can someone who is blind to Being be anything but blind to God?"[21]

---

21. *My Work,* p. 85. An elegant defense of the metaphysics of Being in the

The completion of this pre-comprehension is delineated only in the history of salvation illustrated in *The Old Covenant* (vol. VI) and the *New Covenant* (vol. VII), where the glory of God in its full form is described according to the triple scansion of *epiphany,* as God's being with us, of *poiesis,* as the justification worked by the glorious *kenosis* of Christ, and finally of *charis.* The two volumes dedicated to *Clerical Styles* (vol. II) and *Lay Styles* (vol. III), about which we have already spoken, are the thematic development of how in Christian thought glory has left its traces in forms which are still significant today.

Thus, in the progression from the first to the last volume we move from an aesthetic understood in a Kantian sense as a theory of perception to a theological aesthetic which in its full sense is like the self-presentation of the glory of God which carries in itself its own evidence and manifests it to the eyes of the faithful. The twofold movement of response to the appearance of the form, that of perception and of asceticism, in the end fuses into a single movement: one lives only in the other. We cannot be mere spectators of glory, but we are seized by it in order to become its co-workers.

This assures passage to the second installment of the Trilogy, the Dramatics. "Anyone who took seriously the encounter described in the aesthetics was obliged to see that the phenomenon presented to him was one in which he had always been involved."[22] While it was ecstasy which nested in the aspect of vision, here it is necessary to pass to the dramatic movement which characterizes existence even at the

---

contemporary world can be found in *The Glory of the Lord, vol. V: The Realm of Metaphysics in the Modern Age,* p. 648, where one reads:

> The Christians of today, living in a night which is deeper than that of the Later Middle Ages, are given the task of performing the act of affirming Being, unperturbed by the darkness and the distortion, in a way that is vicarious and representative for all humanity: an act which is at first theological, but which contains within itself the whole dimension of the metaphysical act of the affirmation of Being. . . . But in so far as they are to shine "like the stars in the sky," they are also entrusted with the task of bringing light to those areas of Being which are in darkness so that its primal light may shine anew not only upon them but also upon the whole world; for it is only in this light that man can walk in accordance with what he is truly called to be.

22. *Theo-Drama: Theological Dramatic Theory, vol. I: Prolegomena,* trans. Graham Harrison (San Francisco, 1988), p. 15.

natural level, inasmuch as not even the slightest attempt at self-understanding on the part of men occurs except from within his *actual existence*. But what is man's dramatic existence except a question thrown into being? A question which reveals to the attentive eye that it has always been included in the action of its maker? Thus, the drama becomes precisely that: God's action. "Now we must allow the encountering reality to speak in its own tongue or, rather, let ourselves be drawn into its dramatic arena. For God's revelation is not an object to be looked at: it is his action in and upon the world, and the world can only respond, and hence 'understand,' through action on *its* part."[23]

If this action is inevitably the encounter of two freedoms as radically dissimilar as infinite and finite freedom, which at the same time communicate and are not devoid of a certain analogy, what will happen when finite freedom obstinately attempts to take the path of self-salvation? God will freely desire to plunge himself into the drama and become its protagonist, who fights in person the mortal battle *(mors et vita duello conflixere mirando)*, in a theodrama which reopens to man's freedom space in which to follow him, a space for an imitation which is possible only by the gratuitous act of incorporation to Christ in the Church.

In the permanent actuality of Christ's response to the drama, there is a revelation for men of every age of the unfathomable mystery of the Triune God and of the events which await us when the figure of this passing world will come to an end.

After the long trek in search of dramatic instruments in the *Prolegomena* (vol. I), Balthasar studies the *dramatis personae*. The players are seen first in God, as if Balthasar wanted to describe each personage before it comes on the scene, but with the awareness that only the action can reveal the identity of the individual actors. *Man in God* (vol. II) is designed to identify the *dramatis personae* in this fashion, offering us a singular anthropology, in which, in complete conformity with the already established theoretical principle that in contingent being the transcendentals occur only within a polarity, a dramatic quality is revealed even *in naturalibus*, nor will it be automatically dissolved even with the entrance of the Protagonist on the scene.

He is discussed in *Man in Christ* (vol. III), where the principle of the identity of person and mission not only governs the formation of

23. Ibid.

a Christology in which the drama is concentrated in the Johannine *hour*, but also permits the development of a mariological and ecclesiological dynamic.

The *Action* (vol. IV) is the soteriological description of the decisive battle in the drama. Conducted with the meticulous purpose of regaining the notion of vicarious substitution, it closes with the attempt at a christological theology of history.

Lastly, *The Final Act* (vol. V) allows us a certain penetration into the deepest mysteries of the Trinity and of eschatology. The intent here is to reveal traces of the resplendent countenance of the God whom Jesus of Nazareth, speaking of his relationship with the Father and with the Spirit, has revealed to the faith. We see him only as in a mirror against all the claims of absolute idealism. He continually eludes us ("Try to understand, God is not like this!") during this time of momentary tribulation, even though believers in Christ are allowed, more than even Moses, to walk, even to run (see Phil. 3:12), as if they saw the Invisible.

Of the entire Trilogy, the Dramatics is certainly the part which attempts to articulate in a highly original manner, and not without constant reference to the history of theology, an *intellectus fidei* of the totality of Christian revelation. The question Balthasar puts to himself then arises naturally: "What, after all this, is the point of a *Theologic?*"[24] The reason for this is twofold: in the first two panels of the triptych the fact of revelation was presupposed as a given and, as such, capable of being comprehended and imitated by men. But how will God be able to make himself comprehensible to men in human terms without losing his identity in some emanationistic schema? And how can man's limited spirit grasp the unlimited meaning of the incarnate Word? This is the question of truth posed in all the fullness of its articulations.

Balthasar first of all approaches the question from below in *The Truth of the World* (vol. I). Here, the theme is studied from within contingent being, as usual with the help of the doctrine of the analogy of the transcendentals. Just as for the other transcendentals, in the world of contingent being the principle of polarization, of the "rigorous intertwining of the poles of tension,"[25] holds good as well.

24. *Theologik*, I:XXI.
25. Ibid., p. 110.

Thus, the polarity of object and subject is delineated on the plane of *truth as nature,* and is duplicated on the plane of *truth as liberty.* The same polarity reappears (although on a higher level) in *truth as mystery* on account of the dynamism of unveiling and veiling inherent in mystery. And it serves as prelude to fulfillment in the form of *truth as participation,* in which, however, there remains a polarity of finitude and infinity.

The way of truth will thus have to be undertaken anew by accepting the apparently still more radical challenge of the God-Man or Man-God. This is the task of *The Truth of God* (vol. II). How can the two natures of Christ coexist? Is this not a still more extreme paradox than that of the polarity of truth in the sphere of the contingent? "Can we conceive of a being capable of realizing in itself the transposition from archetype to image without falsifying the former?"[26] If we consider that this transposition occurs between *verbum* and *caro* and the *caro* is the *caro peccati,* where every similitude must yield to "greater dissimilitude" (DS 806), how can we conceive that the Word is able to translate itself into flesh? The question is absolutely crucial and requires a reflection in both directions of the analogy: the ascending direction (ana-logic) which moves from the image to the archetype and the descending direction (cata-logic), which moves from the archetype to the image. Balthasar is assisted in his enterprise by Triadology and Christology, as well as by a good number of facts of eschatology proposed in *Theo-Drama.* Beginning with John's concept of *truth* and suggesting the hypothesis of Trinitarian ontology and logic (ontology and logic of love), Balthasar studies identity and difference in God and in the creature. The conclusion, which we only allude to here before taking it up again thematically, is as follows:

> God is one, good, true, and beautiful because he is essentially Love, and Love presupposes the One, the Other and their unity. And if it is necessary to suppose the Other, the Word, the Son, in God, then the otherness of the creation is not a fall, a disgrace, but an image of God, even as it is not God. And as the Son in God is the eternal icon of the Father, he can without contradiction assume in Himself the image that is the creation, purify it and make it enter into the communion of the divine life.[27]

26. Ibid., p. XVII.
27. *My Work,* p. 118.

In the profound unity of the dogma of the Trinity and of the Incarnation the basis is thus laid for the response, which is at first left in suspense, to the great question of why God, who did not need it, created the world.

But all this could not be understood by man if the *Geist der Wahrheit* (Spirit of Truth) (vol. III) did not introduce the limited human spirit to the comprehension of the logic of the Logos. He who is sent in intimate unity with the Son interprets for the Church, as the credo teaches us, the central truths of Christian salvation: the Church itself, the sacraments, the resurrection of the flesh, and eternal life.[28]

Form, drama, and logos — these are the keys upon which Balthasar relies to fill out the analogy of the transcendentals between the Being who is subsistent (God) and contingent being. He does so keeping before him the total horizon of being just as God himself wanted to reveal it. With his child's faith intact, even after and during his Ignatian-Johannine call and the task he shared with Adrienne *(Unser Auftrag)* he proceeds as one struck by the beauty of the supreme Form who never refused to act within it and with it, gazing with simple eyes upon the visible signs of the logic of the faith.

Balthasar's theology, whose contents now require some illustration, stems from this attitude. However, a final, necessary word of introduction must be said if we are to grasp its originating source in all the wealth of its implications.

---

28. Balthasar's thought on the subject can also be studied in *Credo: Meditations on the Apostles' Creed* (New York, 1990).

CHAPTER FIVE

The Chief Bases of the Theological Method II. Christocentrism

"To display the Christian message in its unsurpassable greatness *id quo maius cogitari nequit* because it is . . . God's deepest love in the splendor of his dying so that all might live beyond themselves for him."[1] Christ as the point of origin and the ultimate horizon is, in the whole of Balthasar's vision, the explicit program which he continually propounded from the beginning to the end of his life.[2]

Here we intend to examine more closely the contours of this Christocentrism, to grasp its theological significance from the point of view of all of Balthasar's writings. If we speak of a Christocentric horizon, this signifies that our interest focuses primarily on method and not on content. This content, rather, will be found under the title *Christology,* even if, as we have often repeated, the form of Balthasar's theology eludes any attempt improperly to separate content and method.

It could be said, then, that Christocentrism indicates the point of

---

1. *My Work,* p. 50.
2. Ibid., p. 50. For the beginning of his life, see Balthasar's *Apokalypse der deutschen Seele,* 3 vols. (Salzburg, 1937-1939), where "the eschatological thinking of German writers was depicted in the light of Christ." Ibid., p. 50. For the end of Balthasar's life see the remark tinged with sorrow for the world: "Humanity will prefer to renounce all philosophical questions — in Marxism, or positivism of all stripes, rather than accept a philosophy that finds its final response only in the revelation of Christ." Ibid., p. 118.

view from which to contemplate revelation. How can we describe this perspective in Balthasar?

As early as 1948,[3] in a text that has become a classic statement of his theology, Balthasar could shed light with a profound and unified Christocentric vision on the vexed question of the relationship between nature and grace:

> Human nature and its mental faculties are given their true center when in Christ; in him they attain their final truth, for such was the will of God the Creator from eternity. Man, therefore, in investigating the relationship *between* nature and supernature has no need to abandon the standpoint of faith, to set himself up as the mediator between God and the world, between revelation and reason, or to cast himself in the role of judge *over* that relationship. All that is necessary is for him to understand "the one mediator between God and man, the man Jesus Christ" (1 Tim. 2:5), and to believe him in whom "were all things created in heaven and on earth . . . all by him and in him" (Col. 1:16). Christ did not leave the Father when he became man to bring all creation to fulfillment; and neither does the Christian need to leave his center in Christ in order to mediate him to the world, to understand his relation to the world, to build a bridge between revelation and nature, philosophy and theology.[4]

From this text, a concept of the relationship between nature and grace emerges which overcomes any extraneousness between the two terms, without going so far as to nullify the legitimate autonomy of nature and, correlatively, of reason. It is simply that nature is seen in Christocentric terms: not as a presupposition extrinsic to grace but as internal to it, internal but distinct. If grace, in the one real historical order, is not a *superadditum* of nature, then inevitably the latter must be thought of as a dimension, a component of that Christic whole which is grace.

An easily negotiable way to trace Balthasar's theological trajectory in the matter of Christocentrism is to show the weight of the work of de Lubac and of Barth in the formation of his own thought: de Lubac with the great question of the link between nature and grace; Barth with his "universalist doctrine of predestination."[5]

---

3. C. Capol, *Bibliographie,* p. 41, no. 62.
4. "Theology and Sanctity," pp. 194-95.
5. *My Work,* p. 50.

The importance of the question in the theological debate which took place in the middle of this century is well known, as is its verification — but not its impossible failure[6] — in the period surrounding Vatican Council II, within the problematic of Christ's place in the actual-historical reality of the salvation of man and the world.

By way of a very brief synthesis we can say first of all that Balthasar makes his own the conviction which emerged from the "microscopic studies" of his authoritative friend de Lubac that Catholic theology must decide to accept a more dialectical view of the idea of nature.[7] In fact, in a certain sense Balthasar considers as too subtle the distinctions made by the French Cardinal between the creation of the spiritual being and the supernatural finality of its nature on the one hand, and the free offer of divine participation on the other: "Do not one and two coincide conceptually? And if one thinks theologically from the starting point of the unity of God's salvific plan, is not the whole an indivisible act of God's freedom that — *in ordine executionis* — can only be conceptually analyzed into two moments?"[8]

It already appears necessary, in order to solve the problem, to leave behind the plane of hypothesis and to place ourselves squarely on the real historical plane where man concretely finds himself. This means to abandon false qustions whose real origin is the demand to know that which, in *ordo existentiae,* can only be left to God.[9] We must, in fact, limit ourselves to the experience of the real world, of nature as it actually is, and of the real impossibility that it may earn grace. If we place ourselves on this plane it is not difficult to accept the validity of the conviction held by a host of Catholic theologians from Przywara to Guardini, Schmaus, and Pieper — just to indicate that this is not at all a superficial position for Balthasar — for whom grace does not denote something

6. "Three years later [*Athéisme et sens de l'homme* (Paris, 1968)], de Lubac will describe the whole 'nature-supernatural' terminology as 'not particularly felicitous.' Today many prefer to speak . . . of the 'Mystery of Christ.' What is essential is that in the meantime people have learned to think in more decidedly personal categories. And yet the underlying question is not simply a relic of the past; the modern secularism within the Church has made it again quite relevant." *The Theology of Henri de Lubac* (San Francisco, 1991), p. 68. The same concept had already been expressed in *The Theology of Karl Barth,* pp. 295ff.

7. *My Work,* p. 63.

8. *The Theology of Henri de Lubac,* p. 72n.

9. *The Theology of Karl Barth.*

which would be added to an already completed man but is the form in which man is definitively himself.

Man is thus the simultaneous outcome of a *twofold gratuitous act of God* inherent in the gift of creation. He receives being from God at the very moment in which he receives the invitation to participate in divine life (elevation):

> God undertook that first communication of his being, whereby finite, self-aware, free beings were created, with a view to a "second" act of freedom whereby he would initiate them into the mysteries of his own life and freely fulfill the promise latent in the infinite act that realizes Being. This "second" act does not need to be temporarily distinct from the first: the final cause, since it is the first and all-embracing cause, includes all the articulations of the efficient cause — that is, the world's coming-to-be and God's becoming man.[10]

Nature and the supernatural thus must no longer be conceived as if extrinsic to each other; rather, the supernatural enfolds the natural. The supernatural is a whole which implies the natural as an ingredient endowed with its own autonomous constitution. Balthasar insists on this emphatically in order to overcome every danger of a narrow Barthian approach — for which nature is absorbed by grace — which would be alien to the Catholic form of thought. The intent of the pronouncement of *Humani Generis,* which Balthasar carefully examines together with the entire history of the problem of nature and the supernatural,[11] must be respected in its entirety.[12] "One can very much maintain at one and the same time that the why and wherefore of nature are grace . . . that the wherefore of reason is faith (or, more exactly, the beatific vision of God, of which faith is but the veiled beginning), and, at the same time, that reason has its own structure and legitimacy."[13]

Once the nature/grace relationship (and, derivatively, the relationship between faith and reason and between philosophy and theology) had been stated not in extrinsic, but inclusive terms, Balthasar's sensibility, sharpened by close discussion with Barth, could not stop at the formal aspect of the problem, however essential.

10. *Theo-Drama,* II:400-401.
11. *The Theology of Karl Barth,* pp. 267ff.
12. Ibid., p. 344.
13. Ibid., pp. 382-83.

The question of predestination, which had been redefined by Barth in a new light in comparison to the ancient *infra- or supralapsarian querelles (ante* or *post praevisa merita),* poses the problem of Christ, of his place in the entire plan of salvation, of his centrality. Of Barth's thesis of *praedestinatio gemina,*[14] Balthasar retains the principle of the universality of salvation in Jesus Christ without, however, reverting, in the terms of a classical doctrine of predestination, to the question of *electio* and *reprobatio,* even if these are seen, as in Barth, in the *concretissimum* of the event of Jesus Christ. Balthasar's Christocentric interest is more streamlined and more linear. The theological interpretation of the drama of personal salvation, to which the classic doctrine of predestination pertained, will find its outlets, sometimes harsh and polemical,[15] in other more objective directions tied to the indispensability of the concrete form of Christ.[16]

In what sense, then, is Christ the center of the cosmos and of history for Balthasar? What consequences flow from this fact? First of all it needs to be stated that Christ occupies this position properly, absolutely, and objectively, and not in a derived or partial sense. Free from the narrow meshwork of a Molinistic Christocentrism wherein the reach of the risen Lord does not extend over the entirety of being and of history,[17] Balthasar affirms with great conviction the centrality of the theme of creation in Christ. Beyond the *querelle* between the Thomists and the Scotists on the end of the Incarnation, a question that in the final analysis goes astray on the crooked paths of the claim to penetrate the *futurabilia Dei,*[18] Balthasar joins his friend Przywara in affirming how man, the image of God, is a simple silhouette that finds its luminous figure only in Christ. God, true to his original decree, reveals himself only in Christ, the authentic *ex-egesis* of God himself. Guardini and Schmaus also support Balthasar in illustrating the myriad aspects of this thesis, while

---

14. Ibid., pp. 174-88.

15. *The Moment of Christian Witness (Cordula),* pp. 71-144; *Who Is a Christian,* pp. 7ff.

16. *My Work,* pp. 55-57.

17. A. Scola, "Cristo Lumen Gentium," *Communio* (Italian ed.) (1987):5-17.

18. G. Biffi, *Tu solo Signore: Saggi di teologia inattuale* (Casale, 1987), pp. 21-41. This drastic judgment does not imply a denial that the hypothetical query indirectly poses the question (which in itself is important) of the purpose of the Incarnation. It would, however, be more rigorous to pose it in direct terms.

Mersch places the subject once more in the light of the fathers and of early scholasticism.[19]

The thesis of creation in Christ, however, will find its most adequate foundation only in the *Theo-Drama,* when Balthasar takes up the theme of creation by the Trinity. Taking up again a thesis of Bonaventure, which Thomas also shared in part, he asserts that a nontrinitarian God could not have created.[20]

"Necessarily, if there is a production of the dissimilar, the production of the similar is understood as its prior condition. . . . Inequalities originate, in fact, from equality," Bonaventure writes.[21] And he adds, "God would never have been able to generate the creature by force of his will, if he had not already generated the Son by force of his nature."[22]

Thomas echoes Bonaventure in several passages of the *Scriptum,* of the *De Potentia,* and in the famous question 45 of the *Prima pars* of the *Summa* with the thesis that the Trinity is the principle of order *(principium ordinis)* of creation, since the processions of the Persons in God are, in a certain sense, the cause and the reason of the procession of creatures from God.[23]

It will not be without profit to recall here, by way of parenthesis, that Balthasar lays down this theme as a condition for answering the great question which arises from man's consciousness when he observes the fissure between being and essences: Why does God, who does not need the world, create it?[24] Already at an ontological level, yet even more here as we illustrate the Christocentric cipher of all reality, we can perceive Balthasar's trinitarian doctrine begin to take shape through his thesis that triune love allows difference in God himself, even though this difference occurs in the realm of created being.

There is a final step required in order to understand Balthasar's

19. *The Theology of Karl Barth,* pp. 333-34.

20. *Theodramatik, vol. IV: Das Endspiel,* pp. 53-92.

21. "De necessitate si est productio dissimilis praeintelligitur productio similis. . . . Inaequalitates oriuntur ex aequalitates." *Hexaemeron,* XI:9.

22. In *I Sent.,* d. 7, dub. 2.

23. See especially the two passages of the *Summa:* I, q.45, a.6 co and ad 2um. The entire question has been studied in detail by G. Marengo, *Il principio trinitario della creazione in S. Tommaso* (Rome, 1990).

24. The development of the question, which is at the heart of the problem of the real distinction, known in modern times as ontological difference, is proposed by Balthasar in *My Work,* pp. 111-19.

Christocentrism. This step is suggested to our investigation by the question of the *uniqueness of Jesus Christ,* a question of decisive importance for contemporary Christology. It is already present in his study of Barth, but it assumes its full dimensions only in the sketch of Christology in the *Theo-Drama* and in the *Theologik.*[26]

In what does the absolute singularity of Jesus Christ consist? In the fact that his humanity is the locus in which the archetype himself, the Son — perfect icon of the Father — transfers himself into the image without ceasing to be the archetype: Jesus Christ is the God-man. And this transferal occurs in the flesh of sin, precisely so that the *pro nobis,* our salvation, may be fully realized. Independently of Balthasar's attempt to grasp how this is possible, something which would demonstrate once more the intimate link between Trinity and Christology, Christ's humanity reveals itself as the singular humanity of the Son of God. This humanity is, therefore, the fully realized form of the human. Yesterday, today, and always every man finds in the humanity of Christ the full form with which to compare himself; nothing and no one can escape the grasp of this most concrete event.

All this would be unthinkable if Jesus Christ were not the absolute, original Word, the absolute, primordial self-communication of the Father, the understanding of which is opened to men by the Spirit. Balthasar's thesis of creation in Christ states precisely this. Balthasar thus affirms that man, in accepting from Christ the solution to man's own enigma, is placed dramatically face to face with the necessity of ratifying with his freedom reality as it has been objectively from all time: the beginning is not Adam, but Christ.[27]

Jesus Christ is thus the *Predestined,* and all men are predestined in him.

According to Balthasar, Christ's predestination "is an archetypal predestination"[28] because, as Scripture testifies, Christ came not only as savior of the world but as the bringer of every good (adoption as sons).

25. *Theologik,* II:119-28 (identity and difference in God) and pp. 165-70 (difference in God and in the creature).

26. *Theo-Drama,* III:149-259, especially pp. 220-29 (christological *analogia entis*); *Theologik,* II:201-324, particularly pp. 284-88 (*Verbum-caro* and analogy).

27. *Theo-Drama,* III:33-40, but also pp. 250-59 (Christ's mediation in the creation).

28. Ibid., p. 252.

This can be understood even better by considering the predestination of Christ from the viewpoint of his mission: the preexistence
of Christ, of which Jesus has certainty, is an element implicit in the
totality of his task for the world, a task which, despite its bloodily
dramatic nature, *must* succeed. He is always with God, and even the
flesh he has assumed is part of the original plan.[29] It follows from this
that the mediating role in creation pertains not only to the Logos but
also to Jesus Christ. In fact, only in him could all things be created if
they were to find consummation in him. The archetypal idea of man
is thus found in Jesus Christ dead and risen.[30]

The possibility of becoming *sons in the Son* is given to all, beyond
the mystery of man's free rejection by this divine offer from God: the
mystery of hell and of *hope for all men,* issues which earned Balthasar
so much vituperation to the very end of his life.[31]

It is in the horizon of Christocentrism that the crucially important
problem of the *analogia entis,* which, especially in connection with the
transcendentals, runs throughout Balthasar's entire work, finds its
completion. Discovered in Przywara and submitted to a new, long
reflection in Balthasar's dialogue with Barth, it reaches its dizzying
peak in Christology. The *Verbum-caro,* in fact, in his ineffable, un-
divided and unconfused unity, passes from one pole of the analogy to
the other (God and man), remaining under the law of analogy itself,
without ever nullifying it or going beyond it in a blasphemous idealism
which treats God as a moment in the triad of supreme being and thus
imports the process of history into God himself.[32]

Balthasar's reflection on the place of Christ in the actual-historical
order concludes, therefore, with the thesis of objective Christocentrism, which underlies not only the indispensable, though formal
theme of nature and grace, but also the matters in which the theological content of the question in the strict sense is disclosed: the predestination of Jesus Christ, his uniqueness and preexistence.

---

29. Ibid., p. 255.

30. Ibid., pp. 257-59.

31. *Dare We Hope "That All Men Be Saved" with a Short Discourse on Hell* (San
Francisco, 1988).

32. *Theo-Drama,* III:220ff.; in addition, see Balthasar's critique of Molt-
mannian/Hegelian process theology in *Theodrama, vol. IV: The Action,* pp. 321-28 (on
the essence of vicarious substitution).

CHAPTER SIX

At the Heart of
Christian Revelation
I. The Life of the Triune God

Once again we have been led to mention the two dogmas which constitute Christian revelation: Christ and the Trinity. More than any other Christian truth, which always consists in the organic unity of the whole, these two must be thought out together. They are so intertwined, in fact, that one cannot be deciphered without the other. In like manner, as all the other mysteries of Christianity would, in the end, be incomprehensible without them.

Without the Trinity, how would it be possible to grasp something of what God wished to reveal in the Incarnation, in the cross, or in the resurrection?

On the other hand, how could we even say the word *Trinity* if the *Apostolos* (the one sent), the beloved Son Jesus Christ who became man and died and rose again *pro nobis,* had not communicated it to us? As Thomas says, commenting christologically on a verse from the book of Sirach in the vivid language of the Vulgate,[1] "The Son of God came and he caused the hidden rivers to gush forth, making known the name of the Trinity."[2]

---

1. Sir. 24:40. The text of the Vulgate reads: "Ego sapientia effudi flumina: ego quasi trames aquae immensae defluo: ego quasi fluvius Dorix, et sicut aquaeductus exivi del Paradiso" (I, wisdom, poured forth rivers: I flow like a channel of immense water: I am like the river Dorix, and like an aqueduct I came forth from paradise).

2. "Venit Filius Dei et illa flumina olim occulta effudit nomen Trinitatis publicando. . . ." *I Sent.,* Prologue.

In short, without these two great mysteries, grasped in their ever-lasting interdependence, we could not even understand in any convincing manner why man and the world exist, since we would not be able to answer the central question concerning finite being: How is it possible that God, remaining God and thus not having any need for the world, nonetheless creates it?

We shall not devote any further time to investigating which of the two dogmas, given the discursive nature of human reason, ought to be presented first. We shall begin with the Trinity, agreeing with Balthasar that it allows "us to see together, in a unity, what up to now we saw as a colorful spectrum of broken light."[3] And in fact the mystery of the Triune God stands at the beginning in an absolute sense and thus also at the end, even if it proves to be impossible to state Balthasar's Trinitarian doctrine in a concise synthesis without showing how we can come to say what we say. Thus we shall be compelled to refer continually from within the Trinitarian dogma back to Christology and vice versa. Nor must we forget analogy, and the analogy of transcendentals, which is always at work in his theology.

Actually, it is fitting to begin with a christological question, one which Balthasar considers "the most central and thorniest question of every Christian doctrine of the faith."[4] It coincides with the very essence of the problem of Christ, but it carries within itself the solution to the enigma of finite being. How can the man-God be explained if the *analogia entis* prohibits placing between God and man any concept which, setting itself above God, can unite the two? Does the biblical notion that man is in the image of God represent a sufficiently solid basis to make of him a "conceiver" *(Erfasser)* of the archetype? As a limit concept to indicate the problem: Can we conceive of a being capable of realizing in itself the transposition of the archetype into the image without falsifying the archetype?[5] "How can such a union be

3. "Trinity," in *You Crown the Year with Your Goodness: Sermons through the Liturgical Year* (San Francisco, 1989), pp. 141-45, at p. 141.

4. *Theologik,* I:XVIII.

5. "Throughout the history of Christology, the purpose and meaning of the Incarnation . . . has been portrayed as the transcendent, inner elevation of the image: it is lifted up into the primal, divine image; or the latter is implanted into the former." *Theo-Drama,* III:223.

possible, given the 'abyss' between two different realities that have nothing in common?"[6] Is this hypothesis not a contradiction in terms?

This problem needs to be confronted from every possible side, exploiting all the virtualities of the analogically related terms: *man* and *God*. Analogy will have to be employed in its aspect of ascent from the image to the archetype *(ana-logic)*[7] and in its aspect of descent from the archetype to the image *(cata-logic)*.[8]

A question immediately poses itself: Why begin from the theandric structure of Jesus Christ to speak of the Trinity? The reasons fall into two categories that are diverse but profoundly connected. The first lies in the fact that the event of Jesus Christ realizes the *analogia entis* to the highest degree possible: this makes the figure of Christ the channel of access *par excellence* to the life of God. "The man Jesus is the truth as expression of the Father and, as such truth, is interpreted by the Spirit."[9] This is a conclusion that we reach even by considering the biblical fact that Jesus reveals the Father and the Spirit (the mystery of the Trinity). The second is a still more obvious reason: "We know about the Father, Son and Spirit as divine 'Persons' only through the figure and disposition of Jesus Christ. Thus we can agree with the principle, often enunciated today, that it is only on the basis of the economic Trinity that we can have knowledge of the immanent Trinity and dare to make statements about it."[10]

Balthasar conducts his theological undertaking spirally so that it returns frequently to the same theme and develops his doctrine of the Trinity on the basis of these two continually intertwining criteria: the consideration of Jesus in his connection with the economic Trinity — and of this latter with the immanent Trinity — and the *analogia entis* (in its twofold *analogical* and *catalogical* dimension) expressly focused on the point of greatest perfection — the figure of the man-God.

The mystery of Jesus Christ thus provides the only access to the Trinity. As further proof of this, we can state at once that any other way precludes access to the Trinity[11] and can be of use in understand-

---

6. Ibid.

7. *Theologik*, II:27-57.

8. Ibid., pp. 159-98.

9. Ibid., p. 33.

10. *Theo-Drama*, III:508.

11. *Theologik*, II:117: "No other way of access to the trinitarian Mystery exists than its Revelation in Jesus Christ and in the Holy Spirit, and no proposition con-

ing the revealed aspects of the mystery of the Triune God only in dependence upon the revealing principle Jesus Christ.

What other possibility would man have to speak about God, conceived as Triune? Only the *analogia entis* between God and the creature. As for the *analogical* ascent it is immediately necessary to define rigorously its inviolable limits. Obviously the ascent back from the image to the archetype, if by the latter we mean the Triune God, is not possible on the basis of a consideration of the image itself based purely on philosophy (reason) — which on its own level is very important and is not at all undervalued by Balthasar — or on the Old Testament. Once the existence of the Trinity is known through Jesus Christ, can *analogic* shed light on it? Balthasar here lays down a second important limit. The various expressions of the *analogical* approach — the triadic structure of worldly logic;[12] the images of the Trinity in finite being (Augustine, Richard of Saint Victor);[13] the possibilities of dialectic (Hegel) and of the dialogicians, the students of the I-Thou relationship (Rosenzweig, Buber, Ebners);[14] and the thesis of fecundity which completes the work of the dialogicians (Scheeben)[15] — remain images that look upward from below. Giving a synthetic judgment of this attempt, especially on the part of classical thinkers, Balthasar concludes:

> The images remained as such unrelated and juxtaposed in the creaturely realm, especially those that presented themselves consciously as *imagines Trinitatis:* the point of intersection, in which the lines of Augustine, of Richard and of Scheeben were to meet, could not be drawn even if these latter were extended infinitely. They are images — and here we can include Hegel — which look upward from below and which (an astounding thing at first glance) cannot be used by Christ when he begins to interpret the divine in his person in respect to the human.[16]

---

cerning the immanent Trinity can distance itself even by a hairbreadth from the New Testament basis if it does not want to fall into the void of abstract affirmations having no relevance for the history of salvation."

12. Ibid., pp. 33-35.
13. Ibid., pp. 35-40.
14. Ibid., pp. 40-54.
15. Ibid., pp. 54-57.
16. Ibid., p. 61.

Christ chooses other ways to explain to his followers that he, the Messiah, is man-God. The man Jesus presents himself as the interpreter of the Father: he speaks and reveals himself of his own accord. Thus, the analogy which ascends from man to God must once more cede to Jesus Christ if it wishes to be able to speak of the Trinity.

Only when Christ has revealed the Triune God will it be possible for analogy to say something about it, but it will always have to be on guard against the grave risk of anthropomorphism.

The contribution of *catalogy* may be more significant, especially for the clarification of two essential aspects of Balthasar's Trinitarian doctrine, which are tied to the relationship between the Trinity and the transcendentals[17] and to the problem of difference in God and in the creature.[18] These are two of the most delicate concepts in all of Balthasar's Trinitarian theology. However, in the end this, too, will find in Jesus Christ, who expresses the fullness which comes from God, the point where its explanatory powers reach their maximum.[19]

Jesus Christ, in fact, is the concrete *analogia entis,* because in the unity of his divine and human nature he represents the most exact measure possible of the relationship between God and man.[20] Thus, the *Verbum-caro* is the royal way to contemplate, to the small extent allowed to the eyes of our faith, the unfathomable mystery of the Triune God.

A solid Trinitarian doctrine must, consequently, first of all win access for itself from Jesus to the personal Trinity. For Balthasar this means, in concrete terms, to take the path which leads from Jesus, the man Jesus, to the Father, and thus to the Son, and from Jesus to the Spirit.[21]

17. Ibid., pp. 159-64.

18. Ibid., pp. 165-70. Both sections are actually a succinct survey of the thought of such authors as Rupert of Deutz, Bonaventure, and Thomas among the classics, and Ulrich and Siewerth among contemporaries.

19. Ibid., pp. 171-98. Here, Balthasar presents brief sketches of the thought of authors who have dealt with such interesting themes as Christ the unifier of cosmic polarity (pp. 171-78); Christ the fullness of all the sciences (pp. 178-83); the Trinitarian structure of history (pp. 183-91); and the triad: God, cosmos, man-God (pp. 191-98).

20. *Theo-Drama,* III:223f. The point had already been treated systematically in a long footnote in *Theologie der Geschichte* (Einsiedeln, 1959), pp. 53-54.

21. *Theo-Drama,* III:515-23. The proceeding is taken up again in summary form in *Theologik,* II:117-19. As we have seen, it had already been clearly enunciated in the thesis of the absolute and primordial predestination of Christ, with the passage from mission to preexistence and thus to his central mediation in creation which makes of him, as dead and risen, the very archetype of man (see *Theo-Drama,* III:250-59).

The central fact in Balthasar's entire construction is the concept of "mission." The principle that Balthasar often repeats is taken from Thomas when he states that, for the divine Persons, *processio* (intradivine) and *missio* (extradivine) are the same thing.[22] Thus the connection between Jesus and the Trinity will have to be pursued along this axis which moves from the *missio* to the *processio*. Reflection on the relationship between Jesus and his mission thus acquires capital importance.

At this point, the central christological thesis, to which we shall revert in what follows, presents itself: the coincidence of person and mission in Jesus Christ. This signifies that the emissary *(apostolos)* must know himself from the beginning to be identical with his mission. The profound reason for Balthasar lies in the complex nature of the self-knowledge of Jesus.[23] If he had received his mission only secondarily, it would be impossible to explain the singular consciousness he possesses in affirming that whoever receives him receives Him who sent him, who, in the New Testament, is incontrovertibly the Father. And obviously, one can add here all the verses of the Gospels in which his unity with the Father is forcibly affirmed ("The Father and I are one," John 10:30; "Who sees me sees the Father," John 14:9, etc.). The substance of these passages is included in the concept of mission, which is explicit in the Gospel of John but is firmly grounded in the Synoptics as well.[24]

Consequently, at this point Balthasar affirms: "the world cannot be created without account being taken of this sending of the 'beloved Son'; this means, in turn, that he-who-is-sent cannot be given this mission subsequently, a posteriori, without having been consulted when the original decision was made."[25] But if, on the basis of the texts of the New Testament and of a deep reflection on the self-consciousness of Jesus we necessarily arrive at the identification of person and mission in Christ, "this identity implies that the Son shares divinity with the creating Father."[26] And creation itself cannot have occurred without the knowledge of Christ. We rediscover here the christocentric principle according to which, from before the foundation of the world, Christ was predestined as the emissary. He is the

---

22. Balthasar's comment on the Thomistic texts is found in *Theodramatik, vol. IV: Das Endspiel*, pp. 53-57.

23. *Theo-Drama*, III:163ff.

24. Ibid., pp. 150-54.

25. Ibid., p. 516.

26. Ibid., p. 517.

one in whom the creation took place (John 1:3; 1 Cor. 8:6; Col. 1:16; Heb. 1:2f.).

And Balthasar assumes not only a creator's care for his world but also, in it, love for the world to be created: " We cannot put it off any longer: we must retrace our steps from the God who creates . . . to the Father who generates eternally. For if he-who-is-sent has essentially to reveal the love of him-who-sends, and if he is identical with his divine mission, he must (as the personal bearer of this mission of love) be the divine, that is, eternal offspring of him-who-sends, whom he himself calls 'Father' in a sense that bursts all analogies."[27] Jesus is thus the Son of God generated by the Father.

> Jesus' relation to the Father (to speak only of the Father for now) is not at all the expression and the self-manifestation of his humanity alone but, through the humanity, of his Person which is indivisible from it and which manifests itself through it. The *Son,* as Jesus defines himself, is the eternal Son of the Father who turns to him in his assumed humanity. The *one Lord Jesus* is the 'Logos of God, God from God' (DS 113). . . . The Son, who alone knows the Father in all his truth and who alone is authorized to reveal him as such to men, is not the mere man Jesus, but the trinitarian Son of the Father (Mt. 11:27).[28]

We can now pass from the mission of the Son to the Spirit. "Insofar as Jesus is the fruit of the Spirit's overshadowing of the Virgin, he naturally has the Spirit within him; but insofar as the Spirit is sent down upon him explicitly (in 'bodily form'), the Spirit is 'over him' (. . . Mt. 3:16; Lk. 3:22). John is more precise: the Spirit 'descends and remains' on him (1:33), which does not contradict the . . .'into him' of Mark 1:10."[29] If we consider Jesus as the eternal Son, we can deduce that the Spirit's being in him as man expresses the economic form of the *Filioque,* and that the Spirit above him, who drives him to his mission, is the Spirit who *a Patre procedit,* in the co-spiration of whom the Son himself participates from eternity.

From all this Balthasar concludes: "Only in Jesus Christ do we come to unity and identity in difference, which for the Christian faith refers clearly to the trinitarian mystery. By the simultaneous positing of essential, divine unity and evident distinctions of opposition Jesus

27. Ibid., p. 518.
28. *Theologik,* II:117.
29. *Theo-Drama,* III:520.

provides us with the key to enter the Mystery of the Living God, who reveals his character of mystery only if access is granted to us."[30]

Thus the access from the person of Jesus to the personal Trinity is accomplished. Passage from the economic Trinity to the immanent Trinity is also implied in the second part of this movement. In this regard, however, Balthasar is emphatic in rejecting the axiom that the two are identical. To be sure, the economic Trinity appears as a translation of the immanent Trinity, but the latter "may not be identified with it, for the latter grounds and supports the former."[31]

What can be said at this point of the life which takes place in God? What can the understanding of faith glimpse of what Jesus wished to reveal to us about it?

Presenting Balthasar's thought in an extremely reduced synthesis, we can begin by affirming that the divine essence is not "a rigid block of identity, but rather is something that the Father communicates, the Son receives, and the Father and the Son together give to the Spirit."[32] For Balthasar this signifies that the *aequalitas* among the Persons does not mean a fixed "identity, even if their identity were in a single divine 'essentia' or single absolute 'esse,' in whose concreteness they are identical wherever "their relative opposition does not prevent it."[33] This is all the more the case as this essence cannot be considered a fourth subsistent, inasmuch as each person, who exists as a "moment" in the flow of the processions, is as such identical to the divine essence or being. For Balthasar this implies two fundamental things. Not only does a personal "perennial event" (*Geschehen,* not to be confused in any way with *Werden,* temporal becoming) exist in God, but the being of God must be identical to this "perennial event" as such.[34]

Here we need to interject a long quotation to help us better understand the significance of this statement:

30. *Theologik,* II:119.
31. *Theo-Drama,* III:508. The reference is to K. Rahner.
32. *Theodramatik, vol. IV: Das Endspiel,* p. 66.
33. Ibid., p. 57.
34. Balthasar is not ingenuous and, seeing clearly the difficulties that this thesis could provoke, thus forcefully asserts: "The perennial trinitarian event *(Geschehen)* is much more than a coordination or unregulated series, since expressions such as 'generate,' or 'hear,' or 'cause to proceed,' or 'spirate' express eternal acts, thus real happenings; we must decide to view together these two apparently irreconcilable concepts: eternal or absolute being *and* eternal and absolute event" (ibid., pp. 58-59).

If then the one divine essence is not allowed to act as such in the processions and personal relations, it is evident, just the same, that in these relations and processions we are always dealing with the identical divine Being of every Hypostasis. What the Father, in generating the Son, bestows on him, is the perfect indivisible divinity that He possesses, but He possesses it only in such a way that He, the 'unpreconceivable' begetter, possesses it as given. It can certainly be said that the Father in generating "has not given his substance to the Son in such a way as no longer to have it Himself" (DS 805), but the contrary is just as true: namely, that He remains the eternal Father because He has given all that is His, including His divinity, to the Son (DS 528). And the analogy is true of the Father and of the Son in regard to the procession of the Holy Spirit, who otherwise could not be the same identical God. Does this not signify the disappearance of the last trace of the ever threatening *quaternitas* in God, of an 'essence which persists immovably alongside the processions'? And if we rightly asume that the *taxis* (sequential order) of the processions is indeed irreversible, but wholly outside time, so much so that the proceeding persons, the Son and the Spirit, can and must be thought of as the two who 'allow themselves to be proceeded': does not the essence then become something as equally *in movement* as the very event of the processions? And if the Father's giving of Himself to the Son and the self-giving of both to the Spirit correspond neither to a free choice nor to a necessity but to the intimate essence of God (*'non voluntate nec necessitate, sed natura,'* DS 71), then in the last analysis this most intimate essence — however the processions may be distinguished among themselves — can *only be love.*"[35]

If we assume Balthasar's point of view, the consideration of the essential properties also changes and would have to be revised to situate them in "a hypostatic light"[36] which will show God even more clearly as absolute love.[37]

35. *Theologik*, II:126-27.
36. The expression is Balthasar's own, who explicitly deals with it in ibid., pp. 128-38. In *Theodramatik, vol. V: Das Endspiel*, pp. 57-58, he had taken divine omnipotence as an example:

If we take all this seriously, it would be impossible to mount any consideration of the "divine properties," which [consideration], proceeding solely from the essence or absolute being, excludes the intradivine processions (which happens often in the Treatises *De Deo Uno*). To take an example: We can definitely speak of divine omnipotence in relation to the creation of the world, but we shall also

This illuminates the Trinitarian revelation of Christ, in itself and in its ultimate significance, that God is love. In God, the other is allowed to be. There is a being-other which does not eliminate the unity of the divine Being. A chief truth about God emerges from this whole consideration: it is absolutely good that the other exists.[38] Therefore the identity of God, in a certain sense, tolerates *difference*.[39]

---

need to think, on the basis of the perennial trinitarian event, in what way the Triune God wants to be omni-potent: in such a way that it is not first in creating, but already in generating and spirating, in letting himself be generated and spirated, that he makes over his power to the irreducible other and releases it without any regard for himself. If one wanted to see in this a ("necessary," given the Trinitarian process) "limitation" of God's ever-personal power over himself, hence, a sort of im-potence, it would then be possible to find the point where these two aspects of God's power (as real omnipotence and real transfer of power) are reconciled in the superordinate concept of absolute Love, of which in the final analysis one can speak only on the basis of *De Deo Trino*. The same could be shown for all the properties which are unilaterally attributed to the divine essence.

37. *Theologik,* II:126-28.
38. *Theodramatik, vol. IV: Das Endspiel,* pp. 71-74.
39. The exact meaning of the expression is well explained by Balthasar in *Theologik,* vol. II, pp. 119-38, where he examines the question of identity-difference in God in close discussion with the Trinitarian theology of Augustine, Anselm, and Thomas. He believes that in the use of the Augustinian analogy of the spiritual creature which "thinks" *(verbum)* and wills *(amor)* to describe the processions in God, he can reveal a path which could be perfected through the theme of "difference" in God. He is aided in this by referring to contemporary authors, among whom he is especially fond of Siewerth and Bruaire, who have reflected on the Trinity beginning from Heidegger's concept of the ontological difference (between being and the entity), re-elaborating it radically with the purpose of holding it in line with the requirements of the Trinitarian dogma. For these two the proposition of the onto-logical difference is thoroughly transformed in God, in whom obviously there is no ontological difference in Heidegger's sense, since in God being does not differ from the supreme Entity, but differs *in* him and reveals itself as its own hypostatic difference. The theme of difference permits Balthasar, on one hand, to leave in the background the category of subsistent relation to indicate the Persons, and on the other to conceive differently the connection between essence and hypostasis in terms of the perennial event about which we have spoken. This approach obviously does not remove the speculative impasse innate in any Trinitarian theology (it is impossible for us to hold together in the same statement identity and difference, ibid., p. 124), but we open ourselves to the exigencies of the (Trinitarian) "economy" which induce us to con-sider, in terms of "unpreconceivable" love (p. 126), the perennial event of the cir-cumincession of the processions in the sole essence of God. From this perspective

But how can we imagine the intratrinitarian dynamism concretely? How can we express the perfect reciprocal self-giving of the individual Hypostases, who are necessarily characterized by a divine, absolute self-possession? First of all, there is the Father's giving of himself *(Fons totius divinatis)* to the Son, in which he bestows on him everything that he is (in God there is only being and not having).[40] The Son responds to the Father's total self-giving. And the love which unites the two is so perfect as to spirate the Person of the Spirit, the fulfillment of the co-being of the Father and the Son. Such co-being is not eliminated but eternally presupposed by the Spirit, who eternally manifests its positiveness. To the total gift of self by the Father and by the Son, the Spirit responds by making his own equally total gift of self.

The summary presented here — an inevitable impoverishment of the exuberant richness of Balthasar's trinitarian thought — would not be complete if we did not also state that for Balthasar this total self-giving of the Persons in God is a primordial kenosis, capable both of explaining and of removing any difference existing outside the Trinity.[41]

The perfect intratrinitarian communion that carries in itself this essential element of kenotic otherness (difference), which is linked to the perennial event of love circulating eternally in God, is the adequate explanation not only of the Creation and of the Incarnation *(Verbum-caro),* as we have already noted, but also, as we shall see, of the mortal assumption of the *flesh of sin* in the person of him who, having become a curse for us, allowed himself to be impaled on the ignominious tree of the cross.

In fact, once otherness-difference (kenosis) has been established

---

even the procession of the Word (here is the difference from the classical authors) can be more adequately thought out in terms of love. But if the Father's giving of himself *(Sich-schenken)* to the Son, and of the two to the Spirit, takes place *non voluntate nec necessitate sed natura* (DS 71), then this essence of God, where the processions can always be distinguished one from another, can in the end only be Love (pp. 126-28).

40. Nevertheless, we should not forget here what has already been said about the impossibility of the *intellectus fidei* to hold, in a single proposition, not only the entire mystery but even just one of its constituent aspects (essence, hypostasis); cf. DS 805. He who gives does not lose himself and that which he has given: "Both things must be affirmed together as identical: the authentic, active handing over of one's self which involves the entire Person who is handing himself over — and the eternal being of this Person precisely in the act of handing himself over." *Theodramatik, vol. IV: Das Endspiel,* p. 75.

in God, every other difference can be read catalogically in terms of *kenosis*. The difference involved in the real distinction, which gives rise to the ultimate question why God created the world, is the *kenosis* of the Creation, which is not at all "a fall" from God; the difference of the abyssal transition, within the *analogia entis,* from God the archetype to man the image is the kenosis of the Incarnation; the difference of the incarnate God's assumption of the sinner's total alienation is the saving *kenosis* of the cross.

To faith, which attempts to contemplate the mystery through theological reason, the life of the Triune God appears therefore as the originating source of all the mysteries of the revelation of Jesus Christ, and thus as the adequate horizon for the comprehension of reality in its totality.

CHAPTER SEVEN

At the Heart of Christian Revelation
II. The Event of Jesus Christ

We can no longer put off the question that runs through the whole of Balthasar's theology: Who is Jesus Christ? How are we to render a comprehensible account not only of his life, but also of his unique person, in the face of the dramatic questions which flood our consciousness as *children of modernity?* And, above all, how can it be done without attempting, as do many, to treat him as "a mountain torrent that men attempt to channel into their turbines and so make it serve their own ends"?[1] How are we to explain Christ's claim that now rises up definitively (eschatologically) against the pretension of the world to achieve its own salvation? Who really is he who dares to call himself God?

We have already alluded to Balthasar's attempt to *understand* from within revelation the possibility of the God-Man *(Verbum-caro).* If the Other is to be situated in God, the Word and the Spirit, then the otherness of creation will no longer be a fall, but an image of God. And if the Son, who is the Other, is the perfect icon of the Father, then he will be able to assume in himself, without contradiction, the image (man) to purify it and make it enter into the communion of divine life without dissolving it. Nevertheless, it is not this passage of the Logos from the logic of God to human logic (Theologic), which only the Spirit of truth can illuminate for our limited comprehension, to which we must turn our attention.

The path along which we must now follow Balthasar is marked

---

1. *Theo-Drama,* III:26.

rather by the irruption of God into the drama of history, transforming it into a "Theo-Drama." It is in the sphere of the Dramatics that the principal Player can reveal something of himself and of his mission.[2] It is in dramatic action that the questions continually provoked by his presence become entwined with the pressing questions that man discovers in himself, from within his *Dasein*. There, in the close confrontation between the freedom of God and human freedom, his countenance of mercy which illuminates the enigma of existence comes to light — all the more in that the reflection concerning Christ in the *Theo-Drama,* even if very different from what one would find in a Scholastic treatise, has the merit of dealing synthetically with all the central themes of such a treatise on the basis of the original perspective we have just described. The result is a sketch of Christology of the first order, in which Balthasar openly and rigorously confronts the most acute and crucial exegetical issues for the purpose of a critical understanding of the Mystery.

For Balthasar, a correct methodological approach to the problem of Christ begins with the recognition of the *elliptical* structure of Christology, in its perfect reciprocity between the content of the testimony and the testifying form. Through the eyes of testifying faith we attain knowledge of the incarnate Word of God, but it is the latter who continually molds the faith that testifies. Until the Enlightenment Christology was carried on "pre-critically" within this ellipse, basing its "scientific character" on the correspondence between revelation and faith, which was simply taken for granted. There was no question of having to "guarantee" the legitimacy of the Christian faith before the pretensions of an autonomous reason.

After the question of scientific "verification" or "critical knowledge" arose with modernity, both Enlightenment rationalism and idealistic speculation sought to break the elliptical reciprocity between

---

2. Volumes 3 and 4 of *Theo-Drama* are the privileged *loci* of Balthasar's Christology (whose structure implies soteriology). Nevertheless, of capital importance are also the *Glory of the Lord,* VII (where we find a full-blown Christology developed through the lens of aesthetics, that is, of the completion of Balthasar's doctrine of *form*); *Mysterium Paschale: The Mystery of Easter* (Edinburgh, 1990) (a text that rightly has become quite famous); *Theologik*, II:201-329, and *Theologik*, III:153-200. These are only the most comprehensive and detailed treatments, to which should be added a flood of articles (see C. Capol, *Bibliographie*), among which we shall cite in particular those published in the first volume of the theological sketches: *Verbum-caro*.

revelation and faith in function of a knowledge which stands above both. This is supposedly done by taking the viewpoint of a "neutral observer" from which to survey both poles, that is to say, the pair *epiphany of God–eyes of the faith.*[3]

Lurking behind this endeavor is the strong Enlightenment bias which reduces Christ to a simple individual among other individuals, son only of his own time and separated from us by two thousand years. Even his great ethical stature can only tell us something extraneous and unusable for the conception of morality itself: how, in fact, could "casual historical truths become the proof of necessary truths of reason"?[4] This is Lessing's question, reproposed by Kant and inherited by the Enlightenment.

From Strauss to Bultmann, who were motivated, respectively, by liberal Hegelianism and existentialism, there is a progressive disinterest in the historical person of Jesus, whose intention is precisely to respond to the critique of the Enlightenment, though it accepts the rupture of the ellipse which it presupposes. This occurs, in the case of Strauss, to the detriment of the faith itself, and in the case of Bultmann, with a certain rapprochement of Protestant idealism with orthodoxy, but at the price of an almost total separation between the historical Jesus and the Christ of faith, which reduces to insignificance the Jesus of the Gospels.[5]

A second line of reasoning seeks to answer the Enlightenment question from another direction, which moves from Schleiermacher to Barth. These two propose to remain within the closed ellipse by means of the theory of the correspondence between "the archetype which reconciles" and "the reconciled conscience." The novelty consists in the idea of archetype. For Schleiermacher, Jesus is at the same time a historical individual and the perfect, unique, and unrepeatable archetype of the man imbued with God. When it is preached, an immediate existential relationship springs up between this archetype and the "pious soul which listens."[6] For Barth, the archetype is the

---

3. *Theo-Drama,* III:59.

4. G. E. Lessing, "On the Proof of the Spirit and the Power," in *Nathan the Wise, Minna von Barnhelm, and Other Plays and Writings,* ed. Peter Demetz (New York, 1991), pp. 309-14. The process becomes more rigorous in Kant with the project for "Religion Within the Limits of Reason Alone," *Kant,* presented by Julien Benda (New York and Toronto, 1940), pp. 165ff.

5. *Theo-Drama,* III:59ff.

6. Ibid., p. 61.

Word of God and the reconciled conscience of the believer.[7] Both declare an identity between Jesus Christ and the words of Scripture. But no critical basis is furnished for this identity because all the interest is transferred to the archetype.

The historical Jesus is so pale and formless in the eyes of these writers as to be almost nonexistent. He is relegated inescapably to a particular moment in time, structurally impotent to become the universal basis for the salvation of man.

What path should we take, then, to found critically the ellipse which constitutes Christology?

By what means will we be finally able to rid ourselves of Kant's objection? How are we to give an adequate response to the Bultmannian problem of a total separation between the historical Jesus and the Christ of faith?

We are obliged to begin from this last question, since in fact it constitutes a failed reply to the preceding one.

Post-Bultmannian reflection is characterized by a plurality of forms, but by a single intent — to prove, against Bultmann, a *continuity in the discontinuity* between the historical Jesus and the Christ of faith, and to do so within the by-now-inevitable framework of the critical method in exegesis. The fundamental intuition of Bultmann's own disciples is well summarized in Käsemann's famous thesis of 1953: A *kerygma* which did not concern the historical Jesus would be as if suspended in space and could not demand faith of any kind.[8]

As for the vast range of possibilities existing today of reconciling the requirements of critical exegesis with those of dogma, it suffices to cite two names here: Jeremias and Schürmann, who, by means of minute exegetical reconstructions, confirm the thesis of continuity in discontinuity using different but more objective models than the post-Bultmannians.[9] To these we should add the name of Martin Hengel.[10]

---

7. Ibid., p. 62.

8. E. Käsemann, "Das Problem des historischen Jesus," in idem, *Exegetische Versuche und Besinnungen* (Göttingen, 1970), I:187-214.

9. This judgment is to be found in *Theo-Drama,* III:84f.

10. Balthasar quotes him often, against Bultmann, in his careful negotiation of the exegetical issues that seem to preclude the possibility of grasping the concrete historical form of Jesus Christ. These are pages written by a *lay* exegete, but they shed a great deal of light on the prickly methodological difficulties of the Christology (see ibid., pp. 59-148).

Nevertheless, there is a final obstacle in the way of a definitive, firmly demonstrated solution to the Bultmannian problem. This obstacle, which originates with critical exegesis, once again reproposes the Enlightenment question of time; it concerns the apocalyptic challenge, centering on the relationship between Jesus and the kingdom of God which he preached. Its origin goes back to the end of the last century, but its repercussions are still with us.[11]

By the time we recognize the validity of the thesis of the *continuity* between the historical Jesus and the Christ of faith, another line of inquiry opens up on the element of *discontinuity*. In particular, we can no longer avoid the question of the self-awareness of Jesus in regard to his mission. Was he only "a witness of faith," or did he know that he was something more? What was the purpose of his actions? Jesus tied the presence of the kingdom of God closely to his person. Did he expect its advent already during his life on earth? In what way did he feel the kingdom to be connected to his imminent violent death?[12]

The apocalyptic challenge marked the end of an "atemporal" liberal epoch linked to a Christology of Protestant stamp, constructed independently of the historical Jesus. This challenge, in fact, poses once more, in an acute way, the problem of time in connection with the relationship Jesus-kingdom and the consequent link between the time of Jesus and that of the Church.

To this "agitated question," as he calls it, Balthasar offers the following solution:

> Jesus looks toward his end, an end that implies not only his death but also the "end of the world," and doubtless has something to do with the apocalyptic "imminent" expectation. Indeed, he explicitly asserts that "some" will participate in this event, although it will affect all. Jesus' form differs from the usual apocalyptic expectation: here, in him, what is expected has already come; it is already realizing itself. For Jesus, the "fulfillment" . . . is indivisible (Resurrection/parousia). For the Church, this is not directly realizable, and this in turn calls for the post-Easter bifurcation, which, from the standpoint of him who has "finished his course," permits the "time of the Church" to be incorporated into his own duration.[13]

11. Ibid., pp. 87-101.
12. Ibid., p. 87.
13. Ibid., p. 100 (author's addition in brackets).

We thus understand that the whole earthly life of Jesus, which was entirely dedicated to the will of the Father and, therefore, in itself was lived instant by instant with a profound calm deriving from his abandonment to this certainty, nevertheless reaches objectively toward an acme, toward a "baptism" which prevents it from unfolding sapientially, but makes it assume an apocalyptic tempo. Thus the final judgment regarding the world, a judgment which is, in fact, apocalyptic and which marks the true beginning of the epochal shift to a new world, is entirely absorbed into the very person of Christ, into the time of his life and into his destiny, precisely because he allows the Father's will to dispose of him to the point of becoming a *curse pro nobis.*

Christ, in his temporally limited human existence, must resolve the affairs of the entire world and of the entire time of the world. All of cosmic time is contained in his "hour" and it does not much matter if this time will continue on or not after his death.[14]

What is important to underline is that this dynamism coincides with the life, death, and resurrection of Christ and is not a philosophic-theological discovery. It is his real death, *pro nobis,* which transfers us to the final situation of the coming of the kingdom. It is the singular, unique, and unrepeatable destiny of Jesus which carries him, from within his earthly existence, particularly his death, to take the world up into his "hour" for the purpose of saving it. Only by loosening the eschatological, apocalyptic knot is it possible to balance definitively the dialectic of continuity-discontinuity and thus resolve Bultmann's dilemma. And this is accomplished without evading the results of critical exegesis, but also without accepting from it points which would claim to empty of value the considerable christological reflection already present in the New Testament, regarding it as if it were merely a superstructure imposed by a later postpaschal faith onto the human existence of Jesus.

We find ourselves faced by a significant congruity: the eminently exegetical problem of eschatological expectation prevents the dissolution of the dogmatic significance of New Testament theology, and the content of the latter, the *pro nobis,* illuminates the authentic exegetical significance of the eschatological expectation itself.

The response to the Bultmannian question (constructed from within the most significant facts of critical exegesis) establishes the crucial premise for the solution of the Enlightenment challenge, that is,

14. Ibid., p. 110.

of the problem of time. One final step remains to be taken: What is the relationship between the problem of *time* in Jesus and in his disciples, especially of those who came after the Resurrection, including us today? There is, after all, more than one factor on account of which an uncloseable gap between Jesus and his disciples seems to open up after Easter. If the hour of Jesus is absolutely unique and unrepeatable, what role can it possibly play in the life of his disciples of all ages? Moreover, it is eschatological, and thus concentrates in itself, above time, all the stages of Christ's own existence: life, death, resurrection, exaltation, and return. In this context, what is the significance of the time of the postpaschal church?

Two other great difficulties emerge when next we consider the archetypal value of the existence of Jesus.

If the "hour" is the center, the end of his temporal existence and the beginning of his existence beyond time, how will the postpaschal Church be able to imagine Christ? If the figure of Christ eludes the Church because of its transcendence toward the timeless hour of eternity, how can it still remain readable as a stable and sure form *(Gestalt)*, at the basis of the myriad of hermeneutic attempts and in respect to the laws of human narrative?[15]

At this point it is necessary to formulate a methodological principle. We must acknowledge that the New Testament has a "canonical" function even from the hermeneutical point of view: in the books of the New Testament there exists a self-comprehension of these crucial problems which should be assumed as paradigmatic for all times. Balthasar states:

As far as the New Testament is concerned, the whole Word of God is present in each phase of the divine Revelation in Jesus, although in its temporal and historical mode this Logos lives proleptically in expectation of a *telos:* it looks forward to its own fulfillment. If we wish to grasp it in its developed totality, in the Church's kerygma, we must show how this totality (which becomes intelligible as a result of the *telos* of the Cross and Easter) was already there as a reality developing through history; but we must also show how the latter remains encompassed in the former, as a permanent aspect of it.[16]

15. Balthasar answers this series of queries in ibid., pp. 122-43.
16. Ibid., p. 123.

Thus, after Easter, the disciples receive with the Spirit not only the ability to understand, but also to fit themselves into the space of the life of Jesus, which opens to them from its fullness the possibility of an uninterrupted following, and in this way to fill the duration of the *eschaton* (the end time) living, as Paul's intuition has it, their whole existence in Christ *(en Christoi)*.

The Risen One offers to his disciples in every age both the grace of *following after* him toward the *eschaton,* the *not yet,* and at the same time the certainty of living every moment in peace within the salvation which has *already* been acquired. These are two simultaneous moments which imply each other synergically in the consciousness of time possessed by the primitive community. This consciousness is much more powerful, beyond a different initial distribution of emphases, than a sterile dialectic of present and future. It is a substantial experience which begins with the paschal event, where we are conscious that Jesus is acting by means of his Spirit, in order to arrive, through the Eucharist and the remission of sins, at union with him. The postponement of the event of the parousia does not lead to any crisis in the primitive Church, precisely because of this attitude that holds Christ to be present in the Church today, no less than Jesus was to the apostles then. It is precisely the *en Christoi* which, in the new sacramental (liturgical) logic of time, assumes the function of erasing the distance between past and present, between present and future. Christ is present here and now. We can thus understand why the failure of Paul's hope of seeing Christ's return during his earthly life does not spoil his calm and commitment to the mission which coincides with life, just as for Jesus the dramatic wait for the hour was not an obstacle to living at the moment the will of the Father.

The answer to the problems raised both by the Enlightenment (Lessing-Kant) and by Bultmann passes, in the final analysis, through the recognition of the singularity of the man Jesus. His humanity is that of the Son of God. The human history of Jesus of Nazareth, the only-begotten Son of the Father, is "God's own history." By dint of this singularity, Jesus of Nazareth and his redemptive work possess the characteristics of absoluteness and of definitiveness. For this reason Jesus Christ is the absolute and unique foundation of salvation in all ages and for all men.

In this perspective soteriology ceases to be an appendix to Christology and becomes the horizon in which Christology itself is properly situated. Christ's mission is at the heart of the singularity and absoluteness of the event. It is the pivotal point for the recovery of the entire critico-methodological discussion and for access to reflection on the nature of the singular being of Jesus, on his consciousness and self-consciousness, and finally, on his predestination and preexistence.

Moreover, the controversies concerning Christology *from above* or *from below,* as well as concerning the plurality of Christologies in the New Testament, not only no longer represent obstacles, but appear as the inevitable condition of guaranteeing the transcendence of the content they proclaim. This is so especially because at the root of all the possible hermeneutic approaches stands the confession of faith of the primitive Church, which rests directly on the apostolic authority coming from the Lord raised up in glory.

The conclusion which is reached in this difficult confrontation with the difficulties of exegesis must therefore be the starting point for understanding the identity of Jesus Christ. This understanding revolves around the *pro nobis,* that is, Christ's mission. Balthasar then proceeds to illustrate the fundamental axiom of his Christology: *the identity of person and of mission in Jesus Christ.*[17] From within this horizon he will trace the path back to the two great driving forces behind every reflection on Christ: the mission in its aspect of consciousness[18] and the mission in its aspect of being.[19]

Every true mission supposes two essential traits: the fact of having been sent by someone else, and the relation between the purpose for which one is sent and one's own person, inasmuch as the mission is realized through the emissary's having to be (vocation).

If we look at the prophets, for example, we note a powerful self-awareness of having been sent and, even more, of having been sent "from their mother's womb," that is, in the very structure of their being. The same sort of reading is applied to Christ by the New Testament itself, especially by John, but even by the Synoptics and by the Epistle to the Hebrews (especially 3:2). Christ is the one whom the Father sends for an absolutely unique mission, which presupposes a person and a way of being sent which are likewise unique. The mission depends upon his absolutely unique relationship with the

17. Ibid., pp. 149ff.
18. Ibid., pp. 163ff.
19. Ibid., pp. 202ff.

Father, upon the absolute singularity of his humanity, which is that of the Son of God. By virtue of this singularity, that which in the prophets was correspondence between person and mission, in Christ is absolute identity. In Christ there is no hiatus between what he is and that for which he has been sent.

The deeply rooted basis for this singular uniqueness of Christ resides in the fact that the economic Trinity which he revealed is founded on the immanent Trinity itself. Therefore, proceeding from the mission of Christ which is wholly identical with his person, we deduce that he is the emissary of the Father because, already on the level of the immanent Trinity, he is from the Father, since he proceeds from him by generation. We return to a familiar theme: Christ's *missio* is rooted in the *processio* of the Son from the Father. The a priori postulate of an identity between person and mission in Jesus Christ, "which no human being is able fully to realize in existential terms" or in terms of content, makes it impossible to give us an infallibly accessible psychology of Jesus.[20]

An important question arises at this point. Every human mission implies a process of becoming. Is this also true of Christ's mission? Evidently he is *totally sent in the Incarnation,* and yet there is a journey toward the *hour* — think of the Gospel of John — that cannot not be a part of his mission. How are we to justify this contemporaneous *being* and *becoming* of Christ's mission? We are aided here by what we have already said about the perennial event in God when speaking of the Trinity. The ontological copresence of being and of "perennial event" in the Person of the divine Word, who, saying himself, "happens" while preserving his divinity intact, founds the mission of Jesus as being and as becoming. In fact, if Jesus,

> "this man who is also God . . . also has a *reciprocal* relationship with God, that is, a relationship expressed in terms of genuine life, developing in decisive events," it is clear that both elements — both *being* and *becoming* in the Incarnate One — express a single *being,* which, while we may not call it *becoming,* is the streaming-forth of eternal life, superevent. The dramatic dimension that is part of the definition of the person of Jesus does not belong exclusively to the

20. Ibid., pp. 165f. Balthasar relies on Walter Kasper (*Jesus the Christ,* trans. V. Green [London and New York, 1976]) to confirm this statement.

worldly side of his being: its ultimate presuppositions lie in the divine life itself.[21]

In addressing the delicate problem of the consciousness of Jesus, we must first of all affirm clearly an important fact: in dying he had to know *for whom and why* he was doing it; he had to know the inevitability and the universal salvific consequences of his death on the cross.[22] Nevertheless, it is a knowledge which stands within the paradoxical unity between the having always been and the becoming of his mission and, correspondingly, between the *processio* and the *missio*. Because of this, Jesus leaves the *hour* to the will of the Father and yet proleptically achieves participation in eschatological salvation and thus brings about the advent of the kingdom.

We must now try to draw closer to the mystery of the consciousness of Jesus, tracing lines whose points of true junction will always elude us.[23] Jesus is he who *is*, and always has been, the task of universal salvation, and this expresses his singularity and his divinity. Consequently, however much we may want to grant a space for progressive illumination in Jesus' consciousness, there inheres in it a "moment" that transcends the human horizon of this consciousness. This establishes convergence between the freedom of the Father, who always refers the Son to the necessity of the mission, and that of the Son who always chooses it, against the paths shown to him by the world distant from God.

If the consciousness of Jesus about his absolute mission must coincide with his self-awareness, this means that both this consciousness and this mission are *unpreconceivable*.

Balthasar coins this neologism to indicate how much in the consciousness of Jesus derives from the singular relationship between the Son and the Father and cannot have been conceived of by Jesus himself before and independently of his person, because his self-awareness coincides precisely with the consciousness of his mission.

---

21. *Theo-Drama,* III:158f.

22. Balthasar quite properly reproaches those who attempt to expel this radical fact from the self-consciousness of Jesus and ascribe it to the postpaschal moment (ibid., pp. 163ff.).

23. Balthasar lets us know how ridiculous, not to mention disrespectful, it is to ask ourselves what can transpire in the mind of one who is the Son of God (ibid., p. 165).

And this is dependent on the postulate that in him person and mission coincide.[24] But does this not run counter to the fundamental psychological law that an *awakening thou* is needed to bring the infant to self-consciousness? For Balthasar this opens the way to graft Mariology into the core of Christology. In fact, Mary was uniquely selected beforehand to be the thou who awakens the self-awareness of the infant Jesus, in harmony with its "unpreconceivable" content deriving from his singular relationship of Son to the Father.[25]

The particular structure of the self-awareness of Jesus (which is transcendently "unpreconceivable" yet does not exclude a progressive illumination) finds its presupposition in the economic form assumed by the Trinity. For Balthasar, in fact, there is a *trinitarian inversion* in the economic order, in the sense that Jesus is under the action of the Spirit from the moment of conception; the Spirit is over him.

We are no longer in the order of the immanent Trinity; in fact, in the execution of the mission it is the Spirit who places Jesus' mission before him in a very new situation. "For the Spirit's role is not simply to discover in the man Jesus the appropriate instrument for the Son's historical obedience: it is explicitly to overshadow the Virgin and so bring the Son into the condition of humanity, as the credal formulas clearly affirm. But in this activity on the part of the Spirit, the Son is already obedient, insofar as he entrusts himself to the activity of the Spirit in accord with the Father's will. As we have often stressed, this handing-over of himself is no mere passivity, but a form of action."[26] In the state of glory, the order will return to that of the immanent Trinity. In fact, in the state of glory "the exalted Lord is given manifest power, even in his humanity, to breathe forth the Spirit. Thus the

24. Ibid., pp. 167ff.

25. Balthasar's thesis sets out from the consideration that without an "awakening thou" a child would not really be human: the Incarnation would thereby suffer injury. On the other hand, "it is not necessary (indeed, it would be inappropriate) for the child's consciousness of mission to be imparted and inculcated from outside; all that is necessary is that the initial awakening shall be in harmony (a 'preestablished' harmony) with the specific nature of his self-consciousness (which we cannot conceive as having a starting point). All that is necessary, therefore, is that the child's inner initiation, under the guidance of his eternal Father, shall take place in harmony with his external, historical initiation" (ibid., p. 176). Through grace, then, Mary is conformed to the entirely unique "I" of this child.

26. Ibid., p. 186. The theme is further developed in *Theologik,* III:153-200, where Balthasar elaborates a "Christology of the Spirit."

Spirit is breathed forth into the Church and the world; he is proved to be the true Holy Spirit in that he is the Spirit and interpreter of Christ."[27]

One final word needs to be said about the relationship between the singular self-awareness of Jesus and his *knowledge*. For Balthasar it is a matter of balancing the thought of the Church Fathers on the omniscience of Jesus with his radical obedience to live, in the Spirit, the mission that has come to him from the Father. This must involve a sort of "placing on deposit," with the Father, of that knowledge accessible to him. In this way the mission becomes the criterion for measuring even the extension of Christ's knowledge. And this depends, as we have seen, on a free Trinitarian decision, which implies Jesus' knowledge that he is the Son, but also implies forms of knowing (including ignorance of the hour) which are tied to the unfolding of his mission.

Having grasped (as for us the understanding of faith can do so) Jesus' self-awareness in its two constituent dimensions, Balthasar next seeks to penetrate the *being* of Jesus. Once again the starting point is Jesus' mission.

In this regard the most difficult problem, which has been the subject of agonized speculation for millennia, is undoubtedly the "possible distinction between *nature* and *person*." "Here we have someone who is entirely man . . . ; how then, when he uses the word 'I,' can he be speaking, not as a human person, but as divine? Or, if he also speaks with a human 'I,' how can there not be two persons in him, be they ever so intimately united?"[28]

Responding to this question, Balthasar invests heavily in the distinction between the spiritual subject and the person, through what he calls "the struggle for the theological concept of person."[29] In substance, mission is once again the axis on which Balthasar's thought is articulated. Only the mission makes a person, because it alone confers on the spiritual subject, which is included in the human species, its qualitative singularity. The person, strictly speaking, is thus only *theological*.

27. *Theo-Drama*, III:189.

28. Ibid., p. 202.

29. Ibid., p. 208. The theme is discussed in an ontological context at pp. 203-8, and in historical context at pp. 208-20.

We thus also open a channel for beginning to understand the singular unity of the person of Jesus. If there is identity in him between *who* and *for what reason,* between person and mission, Jesus is not one who carries out a task which he has received but is one who "speaks the personal Word of God."[30] Jesus Christ is entrusted, "unpreconceivably," with his unique and universal mission, and with it the clear knowledge of who he has been from the beginning with God. Since it is a matter of that singular mission which, as we have seen, is the incontrovertible expression of his divinity, there is a divinity received by the one sent. That God receives divinity is not self-contradictory solely if this reception is not only God's gift of participation to a creature (which would identify the human nature of Jesus alone) but also the transmission of divinity to one who is God *(Deum de Deo, lumen de lumine).* Thus, his divine nature is identified. We see, incidentally, the most intimate link between the Triune God and Jesus Christ. In fact, only in the identity of a historical mission with the eternal procession can we understand how the communication of divinity is possible between Persons who are identically God.

Beginning with the mission of Jesus (and because it coincides with his person), the road is thus opened, in light of the Trinity, to intuit gropingly what faith is trying to teach us when it affirms that in Jesus Christ human nature and divine nature exist in a single person. It is a question of that most singular humanity (human nature) of the one sent, whose mission is "unpreconceivably" identical to his person. We understand that such humanity can only be that of the Son of God, namely of one who is God (divine nature). Thus a clue emerges to help us find the unique and unrepeatable *person* of Jesus Christ.

It must be added here that, in the archetypal theological person of Christ, the hope is proclaimed that man may not remain mere individual spiritual subjects, but become persons through a precise mission.

If the possibility of a different relationship between nature and person is won by means of mission, the central question of Christology now comes to the fore. What sort of being belongs to him who possesses a divine nature and a human nature? In fact, the two poles of the paradox contained in the mystery are clear. Either he is a single being; but is not the *analogia entis* (by which God is God and man is

---

30. Ibid., p. 220.

man and which also holds good for the Son of God made man) contrary to this? or else he is a twofold being; but in this case his personal unity is endangered, and the figure of Christ threatens to slip away toward mythology.

According to Balthasar, the christological *analogia entis* demonstrates how the way of Christology follows a narrow and crooked path between Nestorianism and Monophysitism. We must cling to the paradox. Balthasar does not enter greatly into detail concerning the ontological modality by which, at least tentatively, we can conceive the unity of person in Christ in the analogy of two natures.[31] In fact he relies on the thesis of Malmberg, and rounds it out. In each of his creations God communicates himself in proportion to the stature of the creature and the extent to which it becomes autonomous in its freedom.

If the Logos communicates himself, and if this self-communication of God represents the supreme and infinite case of every act of creation, then his human nature is really created (Malmberg's position).

To this Balthasar adds as a necessary component the "moment" of the Trinitarian mission which characterizes the entire existence of Jesus. The doctrine expressed becomes more precise if we consider the analogy between the natural generation of the Son and the free creation of the creature. In fact, on the basis of this analogy, the Son, in assuming his unique mission, at the same time represents the Father before man and the guilt of humanity and its expiation in solidarity with his brothers before the Father. The *analogia entis* has not been removed, but the Trinitarian analogy (Son–perfect Icon of the Father/man in the image of God), seen from the perspective of mission, permits us to attempt a better understanding of the theandric mystery of Christ.

A large step remains to be taken: the proper understanding of the sense of mission as it can be grasped only in the dramatic *hour* of Jesus. The problem is first examined by Balthasar in his study of the articulation of the paschal *Triduum*[32] and is taken up again in the descrip-

---

31. In addition to a brief allusion in the text to Malmberg's position (ibid., p. 224), Balthasar devotes a rather long note to the problem, in which he discusses summarily the position of Thomas and of such Thomists as Patfoort, de la Taille, Rahner, and, yet again, Malmberg.

32. *Mysterium paschale,* esp. pp. 89-140.

tion of the *Action* as the central point in the *Theo-Drama*.[33] Balthasar's purpose is to give an account of the soteriological horizon of Christology, the "scandalous" point of which is not only that God became man but that he became *caro* and *caro peccati*.[34] We know that here Balthasar develops not only a rigorous defense but also an innovative reinterpretation of the Anselmian concept of vicarious substitution.

Balthasar first of all identifies the five indispensable soteriological themes that emerge from a detailed examination of the New Testament: (1) the surrender of God's own Son to the point of his death on the cross; (2) the exchange of places (he allows himself to be reduced to malediction that we may become righteousness); (3) reconciliation as liberation from the slavery of sin and the *restoration of man to freedom;* (4) introduction to the divine, Trinitarian life; and (5) the merciful love of the Father which, beyond any discussion of God's wrath, is the reality to which the entire event of reconciliation must be traced.[35]

Balthasar next surveys in brief synthesis the different interpretative "models" which have succeeded one another in the course of history, showing how their weak point is each time due to forgetting one or another of the five basic New Testament aspects.[36]

We actually see, going to the heart of Balthasar's position, how in the event of the cross the Trinitarian and christological interpretation already discussed is illuminated. Once again the starting point is the Trinity. The soteriological exchange of places has its ontological presupposition in the immanent Trinity. Jesus can be abandoned (but we must not neglect the etymology of the word containing the root *dono:* it is the abandonment of the one who has *donated* himself!) on the strength of the intratrinitarian distance *(otherness)* between Father and Son, which is eternally overcome and confirmed by the Spirit. However frightening the alienation contained in the sinful distance of the world from God may be, it can be annulled, and this can take place only in the *difference* of the divine hypostases. The refusal of the creature resounds in the intradivine difference, and the Son who

---

33. *Theo-Drama,* IV:205-423.

34. The entire second volume of the *Theologik* is dedicated to an in-depth analysis of how the scandal of the *Verbum-caro* is possible (in particular pp. 201-329).

35. *Theo-Drama,* IV:240-44.

36. Ibid., pp. 244-316.

enters into the darkness of this "no" is in the right position to substitute the world, taking upon himself its sins *(stellvertreten)*.

On a primary level it is men who place their sins on Christ, even
if they try to deny it. They are Christians, Jews, and pagans, and from
this point of view confirm the truth of the thesis of the *scapegoat*.[37]
The Jews must *(müssen)* reject Jesus as a blasphemer and the Romans
crucify him as a rebel.

None of this would have served for anything, however, if Jesus
had not been able to accept men's sins voluntarily. This willingness
stems from the mission he had already received from the Father within
the Trinity, especially in the difference between the life that prepares
it and the hour which awaits. Inasmuch as the "hour" is an essential
part of the mission, the Son affirms it and takes it upon himself. But
since this requires an assumption to the very last detail of that which
is "without and against God" (an identification with the shadow of
sinful denial), it can be experienced only as an overexaction of obedience, and thus accepted not by the Son's own will, but as the will
of the Father. The Son does not and cannot desire to identify himself
with the sins of the world but only to accomplish to the utmost the
mission that has been assigned to him.

Here Balthasar reaches the Anselmian theme of spontaneity (the
sponte refers to the will to fulfill the will of the Father).[38] This creates the
impression (Anschein) that it is the Father who places the world's sins on
the Son; in fact, it is the Father who, through the Spirit, makes known
the divine will to the incarnate Son (Trinitarian inversion). However,
this has nothing to do with any overpowering of the Son, but rather with
the expression of impotence perennially joined to omnipotence, which
therefore is more potent than all the powers of the world. Once again
the reference is to the intratrinitarian kenosis (the expression that God's
Being is love): God, in fact, thus allows himself to be "struck" not only
in Christ's humanity, but in his Trinitarian mission. And the om-
nipotent impotence of God's love is revealed in the mystery of the
estrangement *(Entfremdung)* of the crucified one. What Christ experiences on the cross is, thus, the contrary of what is actually taking place.
Here is why John identifies the cross with glory!

37. See ibid., pp. 298-313, for a careful study of the famous thesis of Girard and
of Schwager.

38. Ibid., p. 335.

Substitution must not, therefore, be considered either as a pure meritorious work (Anselm and Rahner) or as an identification of Christ with sin (Luther). The darkness of the sinful state is, however, experienced by Jesus in a manner that cannot be identical to that of sinners who hate God, even though it is darker and deeper because it is found within the deepest intradivine relationship. From this point of view Jesus becomes a "curse" and "sin."[39]

The distance between God and man caused by the godlessness of sin is thus overcome and conquered in the "yes" of the Son. In the loving obedience that leads the Son to extreme abandonment, the most radical reversal takes place: there is a passage from death to eternal life, from extreme distance to extreme nearness. In the resurrection, Jesus Christ, having crossed through the darkness of death and of hell, regains the glory that had been his (John 17:5) and communicates it to the whole of humanity.[40]

The vision of Christ on the cross, the form which glorifies and is glorified in the Easter of resurrection, demonstrates how close the link between the two fundamental mysteries of the Trinity and of Christ is for Balthasar. In actuality all the rest of his theology finds its focal center in this powerful foundation, like a sequence of implications, even though they are equally essential.

---

39. A measure of the realism with which the Christian is called to behold the Crucified, avoiding any form of aestheticism, is offered by Balthasar in *You Crown the Year with Your Goodness,* pp. 76-92. (These are homilies on the subject of Holy Week, Good Friday, and Easter.)

40. *Theo-Drama,* IV:361-67. One should carefully note the following:

All the same, Good Friday is not just the same as Easter: the economic Trinity objectively acts out the drama of the world's alienation. So we should not say that the Cross is nothing other than the ("quasi sacramental") manifestation of God's reconciliation with the world, a reconciliation that is constant, homogeneous and always part of the given: rather, we should say that God, desiring to reconcile the world to himself (and hence himself to the world), acts dramatically in the Son's Cross and Resurrection. This dramatic aspect does not entangle the immanent Trinity in the world's fate, as occurs in mythology, but it *does* lift the latter's fate to the level of the economic Trinity which always presupposes the immanent. This is because the Son's eternal, holy distance from the Father, in the Spirit, forms the basis on which the unholy distance of the world's sin can be transposed into it, can be transcended and overcome by it. The dramatic interplay between God and the world is enacted in the temporal acts of the concrete Christ-event and its consequences: it cannot be reduced to philosophical or timelessly abstract principles. Ibid., p. 362.

These will follow upon one another with measured beat, beginning with the theme of "inclusion" in the risen Lord (existence in Christ).[41] First is Mary, whom we have already seen grafted into the very heart of Christology.[42] Next, on the basis of the Marian duality of mother and bride and of the Spirit of the risen Lord, is the Church: the *(sponsa verbi)* which is solidly anchored in the sacramental structure (especially baptism and the Eucharist), in the mission of the fisherman from Galilee, the irreplaceable cornerstone who is nonetheless docile to the charismatic initiative[43] of Mary and John. The following step is the angels and demons who are also characters of the drama.[44] Last of all comes eschatology.[45]

Since these are implications, they are incomprehensible without going more deeply into the two fundamental mysteries, which for this very reason suffice to present, together with what was said beforehand, the form of Balthasar's theology.

41. *Theo-Drama,* III:230-59.
42. Ibid., pp. 300ff.
43. Ibid., pp. 361ff.
44. Ibid., pp. 465ff.
45. Cf. *Theodramatik, vol. IV: Das Endspiel.*

CHAPTER EIGHT

Dramatic Anthropology

In Balthasar's theology, which, it is worth recalling, sets out to transform metaphysics into meta-anthropology, anthropology occupies a place all its own. Reflection on man is, in fact, the privileged *locus* from which all questions about being and, once it is introduced, about the Christian event itself, are opened. In this sense anthropology in Balthasar's work is more than an implication of the two fundamental dogmas.

In any case, the placement of anthropology explains why Balthasar examines it according to a twofold movement of thought: from below and from above, *in naturalibus* and from within revelation. However, this fact must not mislead us into forgetting the single Christocentric perspective which can never be set aside for any reason.

Moreover, whether from below or from above, anthropology for Balthasar is always dramatic: "If we want to ask about man's 'essence,' we can do so only in the midst of his dramatic performance of existence. There is no other anthropology but the dramatic."[1]

Balthasar begins from below with a detailed analysis of the relationship between infinite and finite freedom.[2] The explanation for this choice lies precisely in the dramatic nature of anthropology. Man, as *actor,* feels himself to be free, but in a paradoxical way. In fact, in what sense can a being whose essence is finite be free? And yet man's freedom is an incontrovertible item in his consciousness, a freedom without limits.

What then is the nature of this freedom which affirms itself originally in the self-awareness of man?

1. *Theo-Drama,* II:335.
2. Ibid., pp. 189-334.

Present to ourselves in the light of being, we possess an inalienable core of freedom that cannot be split open. Corresponding to the nature of being — which is both true and good — this "light," like everything else we shall have to say about freedom, is an indivisibly intellectual and volitive light; it is both an understanding and an affirming, and while it is true that only something that has been understood can be affirmed, the will provides the stimulus to such understanding. . . . However, this primal, secure self-possession is not a self-intuition or grasp of one's essence; it articulates itself only *in and with* the universal opening to all being, leaving itself behind to embrace the knowledge and will of others. . . . So there is a fundamental freedom . . . that enables us to affirm the value of things and reject their defects. . . . Certainly finite freedom, the openness to all being, can only strive for something it perceives as good (having a value) — even if in fact it is evil.[3]

This long quotation from Balthasar contains, although in an extremely condensed form, the structure of finite freedom as it is attested in man's self-consciousness. It is constituted by two factors: the experience of self-possession, and universal openness, the necessity of recognizing the coexistence of men and things. These are two givens, even if the second is not simply "given," inasmuch as it does not determine the ways in which freedom will go out of itself toward the other to attain its own self-realization. We rediscover here the theme of the constitutive polarity of finite being for which we have already encountered the justification in speaking of contingent being and of its transcendental properties. It should be immediately recalled, moreover, that the two poles are irreducible one to the other:

When giving us ethical instructions for the attainment of such freedom, even those who attempt to restrict finite freedom entirely to the pole of self-possession *(autarkeia)* must always urge us toward acquiring indifference to everything else — both to what attracts and to what repels. As for the converse attempts to persuade man that his experience of self-subsistence is an illusion and to train him to overcome this mere appearance *(maya),* they can only destroy the outer, empirical layers of "I"-consciousness, not its inner core.[4]

3. Ibid., pp. 210-11.
4. Ibid., p. 212.

If we consider carefully these two givens cited by Balthasar, we discover that the two fundamental movements of all human freedom are connected to them. In virtue of the first pole, freedom is the capacity for self-movement, for responsibility, and for choice; by virtue of the second it is the capacity for assent, for acceptance, and for obedience. It is important to note that the second dimension is not simple, but bipolar. If, in fact, the modes and degrees of the second dynamism of finite freedom are themselves left to freedom for the sake of self-realization, the fact itself of assent to the coexistence of the other is posited, in correspondence to the pole of self-possession, as a necessity from which man cannot escape.

As for the dimension of self-possession, man knows that he is responsible for his own destiny. Newman went so far as to say that man is the source of the creative spring in the moral world. Regarding the second dimension, that of universal openness, man encounters the necessity of the existence of the other with respect to himself. And this presence of the other draws an assent from him. If man should profess to deny it he would consign himself to ideological fantasy: from imagining himself to be God, grotesquely claiming an infinite freedom for himself, to conceiving himself as engaged in a perennial struggle against his own limitations in order to deny them, without ever succeeding, in a perpetual torment of Tantalus.

The dramatic structure of the I thus springs from within the elementary nature of human freedom. Freedom is dramatic, indeed, because of the twofold constitutive dynamism of self-movement and of assent which governs every human act; it is ultimately the dramatic core of the self in the ontological order.

Balthasar's analysis of finite freedom restates the substance of the achievement of the great tradition of Christian thought. The new accent that he places on it consists, yet again, in the underlining of its dramatic condition.

The nature of finite freedom places us once more before the enigmatic structure of the self; before the fact that in itself it is a request for meaning which reveals the double condition of man's precariousness: man is, but does not have in himself the principle of his being; man is finite (the structure of his freedom reveals this clearly) but he is capable of the infinite.

We can no longer avoid the decisive question: Who is man and whence is man of such a nature? It is necessary to note straightaway that the question is not *about* man, but *of* man. It is one that lies at the heart of freedom and it is only from there, where it is phenomenologically noticeable, that man feels it rise up refracted in the indefinite modalities in which his personal and daily experiences of life are fulfilled.

Man encounters the decisive question of the reason for his existence precisely in the experience of his freedom, inasmuch as it reveals to him the existence of a universal and inexhaustible being, which, to be sure, is the symbol of the Being from which man himself and the cosmos ultimately derive. It is important to note how, even when he is not capable of recognizing the symbolic nature attaching to universal being — in which he participates without exhausting it, insofar as it is the act of being of a particular essence — man all the same encounters in freedom the light of universal being, infinite and unitotal. Even if this being were to remain entirely without determination, man's liberty feels itself in one way or another to be dependent upon it.

It can be said, then, that finite freedom reveals in man the existence of an energy that urges him to enter into the mysterious nature of the real. It makes him understand that the demand for meaning which constitutes him opens before him the agonizing possibility of traversing all the realms of being and at the same time carries him forward into mystery.

Here reason (and thus will), astounded by the revelatory capacity of reality, which witnesses to its own character as sign, opens freedom to the ultimate question concerning the reason for existence and for being as such. As we have seen, this question is the source of the religious sense.

The apex of rational human nature is the religious sense.[5] It matters not if human impatience, incapable of bearing the risk (which calls will and freedom into play) required by the recognition of the mystery as the Supreme Being, will treat the mystery itself by the same standard as the idols mentioned in the Bible. Money, lust, and power are the idols of man who does not recognize or forgets God, Eliot writes. In such a case, in fact, the thirst of reason, the religious sense, although buried under the debris of idolatrous experience, will never be totally extinguished, but always remains open to the possibility of

5. A phenomenological-ontological analysis of the religious sense in all its constitutive factors is magisterially conducted by L. Giussani in his magisterial *The Religious Sense,* pp. 47-147. We are heavily indebted to this analysis.

recognizing the Mystery with a capital M. The more so since the recognition of the existence of God is documented in the course of history as the most widespread of the two possible outcomes of man's finite freedom which stretches dramatically toward its meaning. If anything, what creates a problem for man's freedom is not so much the recognition, in some fashion, of the existence of God, but rather living in the awareness of his presence. The tragedy of man is to live as if God did not exist, as if God were not interesting!

Having found the *whence* of his existence, man finds at the same time also the *whither.* Having found God, the Absolute for whom he longed with all his strength without knowing it *(desiderium naturale),* man becomes fully aware of the dramatic significance of his freedom. He forms a better understanding of its constituent factors. He comes to realize that self-possession cannot be absolute; otherwise the structural openness (assent to coexistence) innate in that very freedom would be trampled. And everything other than himself, even God, would become the means for self-destructive enjoyment. Assent, on the contrary, signifies recognizing that the openness toward the other, at once the sign of a need and of a richness, is the movement out toward beings that are themselves endowed with a center of freedom capable of self-possession. And, in the end, if this opening toward the other as a condition of one's own truth is to be possible, then it will imply recognition of an infinite freedom, the freedom of the mystery, of the Being in dependence upon which finite freedom exists as finite. Like a child in its mother's arms, finite freedom is enveloped on every side by the loving freedom of the infinite.

This is not the place to attempt, even sketchily, an analysis of infinite freedom.[6] But it is appropriate to recall that the central question concerning the relationship between the two liberties is posed within the sphere of such an analysis: If infinite freedom is everything, how can finite freedom coexist with it? This is the existentially sharper variant of another series of questions we have already answered. For Balthasar they are all concentrated in the one most radical question: Why does God create, if he has no need for the creature? An exhaustive response to this question is found only in the two central dogmas of Christian revelation, the Triune God and Jesus Christ. Being unveils its true countenance and allows itself to be called by name only at the heart of Christian revelation.

6. *Theo-Drama,* II:243-84.

It is easier to follow Balthasar in his synthetic sketch of anthropology once we have grasped clearly the significance of human freedom.[7] This involves following him, not only as he moves from below, but also to the point where the insufficiency of a reflection *in naturalibus* urges a change of vantage point. The irruption of Christ into history will then become the full light outlining man's *silhouette:* Jesus, the perfect archetype, will reveal the countenance of man made in his image.

Balthasar's anthropology rests on the principle of polarization as the constituent characteristic of contingent being. This same principle sheds light on the dramatic nature of anthropology.[8]

Man, in fact, is already on stage in the very midst of the action; he is suspended willy-nilly between a "from" and a "to": This given is structurally unalterable and is the sign of his constituent finitude. "Yet . . . he [man] cannot step out of the dramatic action in which he finds himself in order to reflect on which part he will play. He is part of the play without having been asked, and he in fact plays a role. But which role?"[9]

Let us begin with a glance from below. Perceiving himself in action, man registers the existence in himself of a threefold constituent polarity: spirit-body, man-woman, individual-community.

We must observe at once that these three tensions do not exist on the same level. Of the three, the first distinguishes the concrete form of the self: this being endowed with soul and body, which, rooted in the cosmos, recapitulates it in itself and transcends it toward the infinite, revealing contemporaneously the capacity for self-transcendence. The other two polarities are originally inherent in this concrete form of the I.

To avoid misunderstandings, it will be easier if we specify at once that when speaking of constituent polarities according to the intuition supporting Balthasar's ontology of contingent being,[10] we intend neither to succumb to a sort of fundamental pessimism nor in consequence to reject the possibility that man can discover a way to

7. Ibid., pp. 335-429.
8. Ibid., pp. 335-46.
9. Ibid., p. 341.
10. *Theologik,* vol. I. For the most immediately anthropological aspect, see *Theo-Drama,* II:346-94.

stabilize the tensions. If anything, it will be a question of recognizing that this possibility is not in the hands of the contingent creature.

Even less does dramatic anthropology signify that a discussion of man initiated from below cannot attain a universally valid knowledge, such as, for example, that of the great Aristotelian-Thomistic philosophy. We only want to endow with a content of its own the thesis of the dramatic nature of anthropology, which requires recognizing that the self-comprehension of man cannot, by its nature, end except in an open discussion — with an empty space *(creux)*, as Blondel used to say. To state that the discussion on man, commencing from below, cannot not remain open is the same as asserting that it is dramatic. And this threefold polarity, which can be observed in the phenomenal order, is nothing but the expression of that content. In this sense dramatic anthropology appears to be by nature realistic and, therefore, in line with classical anthropology, especially that of St. Thomas.

The first tension is of capital importance and casts all its lights and shadows on the other two as well. It founds the experience of a dual unity within man himself. Through the body, in fact, man feels himself inevitably inserted into the cosmos and participates, with all his sensibility and in conformity to his rational being, in well-established laws of nature. On the other hand, by his spirit he transcends the cosmos in his theoretical and ethico-practical faculties and participates in a spiritual nature endowed with rational rules that he holds in common with other men.[11]

On the phenomenological plane of the self in action, this tension, sometimes evidenced through an often intense contrast between the two poles (spirit and body), is insoluble, even if this does not permit us to reach the conclusion of the impossibility of a rational anthropological study of man as "one" being. This would be opposed by Greek philosophy — which discovered in the Aristotelian notion of *hylomorphism* a crucial point of equilibrium on the matter — and also by the magisterium of the Church, which has decreed with explicit pronouncements the three principal truths connected to this classical anthropology: (1) that man is a unity constituted of soul and of body (DS 1440, 3002); (2) that the soul is through itself and essentially the form of the body (DS 902); and (3) that the soul is spiritual (DS 372, 800, 1440, 2812) and immortal (DS 1440, 2766). These are facts

11. Cf. *Theologik,* vol. I.

necessary to the proper understanding of the Catholic faith on man. It follows that the Church implicitly recognizes that the constitutive polarity of soul and body does not mean the structural impossibility that man can understand himself as one.

On the other hand, the affirmation of the dramatic character of anthropology requires us to acknowledge that, phenomenologically speaking, man experiences in himself this tension because of which his unity, though in itself beyond question, is always, as it were, at risk, cannot be taken for granted and is, as is admitted by the very data of *hylomorphic* anthropology, dual.

Such a primordial structural precariousness exposes man, as history confirms, to the risk of choosing between the one-sided possibilities of a double alternative: he either searches for the stabilizing point of the duality by ascending toward the spirit out of his despised body, or else he plunges himself entirely, and thus spirit-first, into the intracosmic dimension, perhaps anchoring himself to a mythical pre-Christian notion of a divinized cosmos *(theion)*.[12] Spiritualisms and materialisms have historically succeeded one another in the search for the path by which duality might definitively be resolved into unity. Spirit and body thus each take turns playing the role of a pure epiphenomenon of the other.

It is important to note, without thereafter falling into relativisms, that the doctrine of hylomorphism surely represents the rediscovery of a point of equilibrium (the Aristotelian *meson*), but one precisely of a dual unity, which leaves the dramatic experience of tension unaltered, especially since "what seems like a natural polarity is also an unnatural dichotomy."[13] Anthropology must make its reckoning with the *dramatis personae!* "If man is not to resign himself to a narrow Aristotelian 'middle' — in view of the destructiveness of extreme spiritualization and sensualization — he must be given *Lebensraum* in the form of a complete blueprint that will liberate him from this straitening 'middle.' Such a blueprint would have to execute fully both movements without hubris and without degeneration."[14] It would have to descend into the flesh from above, without this descent being a fall, and from below, from the full existence in the flesh, would have to

12. *Theo-Drama*, II:349-55. For the deification of the cosmos, see pp. 346-55.
13. Ibid., p. 358.
14. Ibid., p. 364.

transcend it, raising it up with itself. And in this ascent death itself would have to be crushed. It is here that the theological approach of stabilizing the broken polarities is prefigured.

To this primary experience of dual unity the self in action is compelled immediately to associate a second. Dual unity also accounts for the fact that man inescapably exists, always and only either as male or female.[15] Two facts will suffice to give a rapid synthetic explanation of the sense of this second constitutive tension. No individual human being is ever capable of exhausting by himself the whole of man: the other mode of being man (in respect to his own) is always before him.

The duality of "gender," masculine and feminine, thus presents itself at once inside and outside the I. Better, the I registers within itself a lack that opens it up to an "outside of itself."

Of course, such duality does not impair the autonomous constitution of the I as individual subject. We must be clear about the matter, against every fantastic speculation in pursuit of an impossible dream of androgyny after the manner of Aristophanes in the *Symposium* of Plato. Such a notion of perfect complementarity would in the end relapse into the temptation of androgyny. In this sense the man-woman polarity must not be seen as a dual unity that establishes a symmetrical, obligatory reciprocity between the two.

Rather it testifies to the nonderivative nature of the sexual dimension and thus to the fact that it is a constitutive dynamism of the self in action.[16] At the heart of the dramatic givenness of the I, of the fact

---

15. Ibid., pp. 365ff.

16. Balthasar insists emphatically on the original nature of sexuality. He therefore examines attentively a kind of interpretation of the two creation accounts in Philo and in Gnostic and Manichean circles which influenced certain Greek Fathers. Moreover, this interpretation often resurfaces, particularly in its consequences, on account of the periodic reappearance of revised editions of Gnosis. This reading would radically call into question the thesis of the original nature of sexuality by proposing a double creation. Separating and juxtaposing the two Genesis accounts, and appealing to the fact that in the second Eve is extracted from the sleeping Adam's rib, this position advances the hypothesis of a double creation: a first, in a certain sense ideal, creation which would be non-gendered or androgynous, and a second creation, now concretely existing in the gendered state. Philo asserts that the first account indicates the ideal man, the celestial man, the asexual man conforming to the full image of humanity, while the second account indicates the animal man, fallen man. Consequently, man was in God's image as long as he was the celestial one, and thus the image as such was asexual and beyond the separation of the genders (masculine and

that it has always already been on the scene, this further tension appears as the one that advances the I toward an encounter with the other. Even the fact that man is a synthetic composite of soul and body implied that he had the primordial awareness of being part of a

feminine). Gregory of Nyssa, Origen, Maximus the Confessor, the Damascene, and Scotus Erigena admitted and reelaborated this thesis, setting it in a new, orthodox key based on the doctrine of original sin. Asexual or androgynous creation would be that of the original state, while after sin — and the appearance of shame as a symptom indicative of concupiscence would corroborate this — the creation of sexuality was thought to have occurred. It is not difficult to object at once, from a general point of view, that this interpretation is deeply opposed to the logic of the second account. It would imply a man who at first is satisfied in himself, inasmuch as he was asexual and androgynous, who only after the division of the two sexes begins to feel loneliness and the unsatisfied desire of another. The account affirms instead the contrary. Adam feels himself to be alone and the pairs of animals, presented to him in Paradise so that he may first denominate them and then dominate them, do not assuage this loneliness. In the perspective of Philo's double creation, for Gregory of Nyssa, Adam is the image of the totality of humanity and contains even the archetype of this humanity realized in its perfection, that is, Jesus Christ, an archetype created in an act of totality in and for itself: Gregory does not in fact intend to posit a temporal difference when he speaks of creation in two stages, but rather an ontological fact. It is a question of something that occurs more in the dynamism of the foreknowledge of God than in reality. It needs also to be stated that as things stand, more clearly for Origen, but in the final analysis also for Gregory, the *imago Dei* ended up being located in the highest part of the soul. This is a thesis that would subsequently be taken up anew and expanded by the Augustinian-Thomist tradition, for which the *imago* resides in the *mens*. Consequently, just as in Christ, the perfect image, there exists neither man nor woman (cf. Gal. 3:28), so the archetypal Adam is asexual or androgynous. At the beginning, the very ideal of humanity incarnated in Adam stands before God. Gregory of Nyssa asserts that, since man as creature must freely decide for or against God, and God, foreseeing that man would rebel, the latter was created with sexual characteristics so as to obtain the total unification of humanity by means of sexual reproduction. What can no longer be obtained from the point of view of Adam's archetypal value, according to a sort of multiplication of humanity of angelic type unknown to us, is now laboriously obtained through a sum of the totality of the human species produced sexually. It is important to note, however, that for these writers sexuality is not a consequence of sin but is a rather a distinctive sign of sin. Sexuality, in fact, from an authentic Judeo-Christian perspective, is never linked to a phobia about sex. Any causal connection between sin and sex, presented as a negative consequence of sin, must be excluded. Such a supposition can be found neither in Scripture nor in the tradition. The position of the Cappadocian Fathers recalled here did not originate from any sort of sexual phobia but, if anything, from the attempt to develop the content of a theology of the original state. This theology requires that we hold together factors that seem incompatible from within the present historical situation. In the original state virginity and generation existed together, thus virginity

universal spiritual essence — that of human nature. The discovery of otherness in man is thus not, in itself and of itself, the outcome of the consciousness of himself as a gendered being. Nevertheless, this discovery implies taking up the existence of the body within the act of consciousness in such an unequivocal way that it assumes a decisive importance.

This truly brings the self into play as a unified totality *(corpore et anima unus)*.[17] In fact, the original perception of otherness, contained in the consciousness of existing by an act of being which is incapable of exhausting not only being as such but also the universal essence of man, could still remain open to all the forms of rationalism and idealism documented in the history of thought. In the dual unity apparent in the gendered nature of the I, this is no longer possible without obvious contradictions.

In addition to this first constituent element, the dual unity of man and woman inevitably imposes on man an even more acute self-consciousness of his own being "from" and "to," that is, of his own primordial dependence. By virtue of his gendered nature, in fact, man discovers death through its connection with generation. He is not only an individual who through his participation can never exhaust man's universal essence, but as an individual of the human species he is also bound to death in virtue of sexual generation. The dual unity of man and woman places the I within the circle of the human generations that implacably succeed one another, by means of which the species itself is preserved while exposing the individual to death.[18] The dra-

---

and marriage are linked, while in the historical state there is a reciprocal exclusion between marriage and virginity, especially from the viewpoint of physical generation. Moreover, in the actual historical situation sexuality is linked to death through generation. In nature what is born must die. These Fathers hold to the belief that, even if death appears to be a law of the species, for Catholic dogma it is a consequence of sin (cf. Rom. 5); in the original state one did not die, at least not as he does in the actual historical situation. How then is sexuality compatible with immortality? These are the deep reasons which inspire the Cappadocians to speak of a twofold creation, at least in *mente Dei,* a position that cannot be confused with sexual phobia. The basic texts for understanding Balthasar's analysis of this subject are *The Christian State of Life* (San Francisco, 1983), pp. 92-103 and *Theo-Drama,* II:374ff.

17. GS, 14.

18. *Theo-Drama,* II:374, where Balthasar cites Augustine who, commenting on Psalm 127 (n. 15), asserts: "Were sons born to you to live with you on earth? Will they not rather eject you and be your successors?"

matic nature of human existence here touches one of its zeniths. And we see clearly, precisely in this "being unto death," to what an extent this dramatic character is constitutive.

The dual unity of "gender" can be considered with good reason as the first sign of the final constituent polarity of the drama of the I, that of individual-community. Undoubtedly this latter is already contained as *in nuce* in the former, where it can rise up to consciousness concretely; this final polarity cannot occur immediately from within the first constituent polarity, that of soul-body, which leads rather to the experience of the individual as spiritual subject.

Nevertheless, the individual-community tension, even though it appears in a certain sense to be the most obvious,[19] adds two important facts to the anthropological picture that we are drawing. First of all, it completes the manifestation of dual unity by making us aware of man's primordial social nature. We have arrived at Aristotle's *zoon politikon,* with all the variations of interpretation which have succeeded one another throughout the centuries. Their vast range extends between two extremes: the structurally optimistic extreme of a paradisaical Nature, which constitutes the model of an absolute spontaneity to look back upon as the locus of a nostalgic, however impossible, return; and the structurally pessimistic extreme of the *homo homini lupus,* in which the law *(nomos)* stands before man as completely external, and, what matters most, does so as the conventional outcome of human liberty's initiative for survival.

In another direction, as the outcome of ideological elaboration, this original tension generates the range of social systems, which may vary from liberal individualism to "perfect" communism.

In all these cases the tension between the individual and the community cannot be eliminated. It is in itself the indelible expression of human contingency. Man, as a unified totality, is a self-positing unity who is capable of transcendence, who is capable of transcending the human community to which he belongs, and yet his destiny is inextricably enmeshed with that of all his fellows. Inasmuch as he is an individual, he is perpetually exposed to the risk of being considered as merely a number in an indefinite series in which *one more or one less* appears almost insignificant.[20] For that

19. *Theo-Drama,* II:382.
20. The entire subject is discussed at pp. 382-94.

matter, does not man's being unto death in virtue of the cycle of generation already tell us as much?

The problem of power, as a particularly dramatic aspect, also emerges within the polarity of individual and community. It could already be glimpsed in the man-woman polarity, as an anticipatory sign of community. And, in truth, the forms and variants of affective power can be many and particularly tyrannical. However, it is at the level of the third polarity, individual-society, that the question becomes macroscopic. Here again power can be represented by a broad range of possibilities, from power as service to power as dominion. Here it suffices to remember that power, as the source of ideology, can camouflage itself and become deceitful. It can present itself as service even when it is pure will to power and dominion. It can even deify itself, as has occurred in history.

In addition, within the third polarity — where the question of otherness, of the place of the other, is opened up completely — the historical dimension of human existence is also fully introduced. This is the moment to specify our meaning of "history," which we understand as *res gesta* on the part of human society, inasmuch as it is constituted in the final analysis by free men, who are thus capable of establishing a proportion between the means and the end, the attainment of their destiny. As such it cannot be confused with the fact that man is existentially situated in function of his dramatic nature, because of which we can pose the question of man's essence only in the living act of our existence. This dramatic nature, if anything, is the metaphysical condition of man's historicity.

For Balthasar the question now becomes this: assuming it exists, what is the path man should follow in order to stabilize these tensions? At this juncture the perspective of his anthropological reflection, which had never dispensed with the Christocentric reference point, even if it remained implicit, becomes explicitly that of Christian revelation — no longer anthropology from below, but from above. Here we encounter again, without further discussion of it, the theme of creation as the realization of predestination, a doctrine which expresses Balthasar's objective, or absolute Christocentrism. It becomes important to understand in this context if and in what way Christ can be the path which indicates to man the significance of the drama in which he is living.

To say that Jesus Christ is the center of the cosmos and of history, or more properly, to speak of creation in Christ, signifies that Christ's freedom becomes the central axis for the understanding of human freedom and that the person of Christ, in its singular humanity, is the *form* through which man may be understood. It is the normative exemplar of freedom and the form of all those who are predestined to be sons of God in him.

In Christ, through the mystery of the hypostatic union, finite freedom is enveloped, *"indivise et inconfuse,"* in the infinite freedom of the Son of God. In this way, through the benefit of the Incarnation, the great story of God's accompaniment of man in the bond of love with the Holy Spirit is placed before our eyes. The freedom of Christ turns toward the freedom of man, which, it must not be forgotten, is a given which necessarily "conspires" with the grace-filled will of God to bring about the actuation of the economy of predestination: without freedom the full participation of created being in Trinitarian life would not be possible since man can oppose his free refusal to Christ's universal saving will.

What is the relationship between the freedom of Christ and the dramatic freedom of man? What is Christ's relationship to man? By way of synthesis we could say that Christ, revealing himself to be true man and true God, through the events of his life and resurrection *resolves the enigma of man but does not settle the drama in advance.*[21] For one thing, Christ reveals himself as the true beginning of man. He, not Adam, is the head of man, the center of the cosmos and of history. The passage from the alpha-Adam to the alpha-Christ becomes necessary. In this sense Christ is he who fully reveals man to man, because he resolves man's enigma; he is the answer to the radical questions of the religious sense regarding the beginning and end. In fact, he reveals himself to be the reply to the question which man is. The reply paradoxically precedes the question and permits it to be posed as a question.

Thus, in Christ, man's constituent tensions also find an outlet, a stability.[22]

The primordial tension of soul and body finds its full significance in the dogma of the resurrection from the dead, which is the outcome of Christ's death *pro nobis.* The microcosmic nature that constitutes man

---

21. *Theo-Drama,* III:33ff. I have already discussed this in "Con Cristo al cuore dell'uomo," *Synesis* 6 (1989): 47-61.

22. Several fine pages on the stabilization of the tensions can be read in *Theological Anthropology* (New York, 1967), pp. 306-30, even though the scheme of polarity treated here is Fessard's (man-woman, Jew-pagan, servant-master). In *Theo-Drama* Balthasar will choose to concentrate on the three polarities examined.

is in this way saved to the end, and the body becomes, in a certain sense, the sacrament of man. It is the factor which, visibly attesting man's difference with respect to the other *"animalia,"* reveals his spiritual nature, which as such remains the unifying apex of the self.[23]

The man-woman polarity is linked to the mystery of the Christ-Church relationship (Eph. 5), where nuptial love not only reaches its fullest *form,* but where at the same time its connection with death through the closed circle of generations for the sake of the species is broken. This is so not only because death is conquered in Christ, but also and more precisely because Christ inaugurates a new form of fruitfulness which is not identical to human procreation. This is a fecundity for the kingdom, which becomes the eschatological sign of the marriage between Christ and the Church; it is a virginal fecundity or nuptiality which is not at all asexual.

Finally, the individual-community tension finds its point of stability in the experience of *communio,* and above all in its zenith, the *communio sanctorum.* It is in ecclesial communion, in fact, that man encounters his personalizing mission and becomes a theological person. The third polarity thus finds in the community, and therefore in the *other* who constitutes it, an abundant source of reconciliation: it is the only place in which man's freedom is maintained in the original posture of self-possession because it is open to the reception of the creative initiative of infinite freedom.[24]

Nevertheless, the solution of the enigma brought by Christ, with the consequent stabilization of man's constituent tensions, *does not signify in any way the anticipatory solution of the drama of man.* The gift of Christ is offered to freedom, which in this sense "con-spires" with grace in the realization of the original predestinating plan. In the Christian life, the constituent drama is not removed. In fact, in a certain manner it is radicalized. The natural tensions are in a sense radicalized in a supertension proceeding from the flooding in of a new consciousness on the part of man. Now he understands better his nature of being suspended between God and nothing, of being someone who owes everything to the initiative of God who draws him up from nothing.[25]

---

23. John Paul II has discussed the subject in his famous nuptial catechesis *Uomo e donna lo creò,* 2nd ed. (Rome, 1987), pp. 27-108.

24. *Theo-Drama,* II:407ff.

25. Ibid., pp. 398ff.

If, in fact, it is true that revelation demonstrates the necessity of passing from Adam as beginning to Christ, this transition nevertheless must always be ratified by man's freedom. And not just once and for all, but every time — from within all the situations and circumstances that constitute the normal texture of human existence. This means that the constituent tensions are not diminished for the Christian but must be traversed dramatically by his freedom. But this liberty is no longer at the mercy of his enigma, but rather is in the tender and firm embrace of Christ, who, as true man, was the first to traverse the tensions of being. This "must" becomes the expression of the demanding radicalness of the Christian life, in which "the everyday becomes heroic."

A decision for existence in Christ, then, does not proceed first in the direction of exacting precepts (a thing that, in a sense, could even seem reassuring);[26] but rather in the direction of the total *risk* of humble adherence *(tapeinos)* to a presence which proposes (but does not impose) itself to freedom as alone capable of resolving its enigma.

The gospel is full of tokens of this new, more radical dramatic solicitation of freedom in the Christian, from the "go and sell everything that you possess" spoken by Jesus to the rich young man, to the "whoever does not hate wife, father, mother for my sake" of the Synoptics. The following of Christ is always dramatic. It suffices to think of the disciples in the painful moments of the Passion: "I will strike the shepherd, and the sheep of the flock will be scattered" (Zech. 13:7; Matt. 26:31). What must have transpired in the hearts of Peter, James, and John when they could not stay awake in the garden? Or in Peter's heart during the bewildering moment of the betrayal? Or in the heart of the mother of Jesus beneath the cross?

Nevertheless, we must never forget that the Christian drama abides in peace and in the ultimate joy of the resolution of the enigma, of mercy. It is because Christ attests himself to be he who responds — from a level that is absolutely unforeseeable and brimming with grace — to the deepest needs of man's heart that freedom risks following him. The great encounters with Christ, as they are evidenced in the gospel, are its constant confirmation: the vocation of the apos-

26. See the marvelous pages on the Pelagianism of the pious in Joseph Ratzinger, *To Look on Christ: Exercises in Faith, Hope and Love,* trans. Robert Nowell (New York, 1991), pp. 76-77.

tles; the encounter with the Samaritan woman, the adulteress, the man born blind, Zacchaeus.[27]

The Christian drama is thus for the full realization of the self. The *sequela Christi,* in fact, cannot indicate automatic possession, because what we possess without struggle does not inspire passion and enthusiasm, as is well illustrated by the figure of the older brother in the parable of the prodigal son.

We can thus conclude this brief overview of Balthasar's dramatic anthropology with the assertion of a principle of great importance for the Christian life: Faith does not evacuate the religious sense. If the religious sense is the synthetic expression of man's rational nature, then it represents the humanly complete figure of finite freedom, which gathers in itself the constitutive tensions *in naturalibus.* Faith without the religious sense is only a sort of ethical and pietistic scheme that does not launch its possessor to the boundaries of being, but rather juxtaposes itself to an unresolved humanity. For this reason it is a faith that tends to become closed in on itself, not to communicate itself, and thus, irremediably, to endure the conditioning of the dominant mentality.

Faith nourished by a religious sense, however, achieves the fulfilled form of the Christian life *(en Christoi),* namely, that of man whose freedom is dramatically thrown open to all human conditions, passionately confronted in the humble awareness of belonging, definitively, to the Mystery of God made man.

27. For a description of man's encounter with Christ and of life with him which, in my opinion, is unmatched for its appeal and power, see L. Giussani, *All'origine della pretesa cristiana* (Milan, 1988), pp. 69-134.

CHAPTER NINE

Moral Action: Jesus Christ, the Concrete Universal Norm

The theme of Christian morality in Balthasar's works calls for a word of introduction. Except in a few rare instances, he did not dedicate himself in a specific and direct manner to the subject.[1] Nevertheless, many of his short writings (*Love Alone: The Way of Revelation; The Moment of Christian Witness; Who Is a Christian; Elucidations; New Elucidations; A Short Primer for Unsettled Laymen*), and above all the Trilogy, in particular the *Theo-Drama,* lay a solid basis for a foundation of ethics.

The starting point seems to me to be the central assertion in his "Nine Theses" concerning Christ as the universal concrete norm of every moral action. He is the concrete categorical imperative since he is not only the universal and formal norm, valid for everyone, but also the concrete and personal norm.[2]

Since Christ fully accomplished the will of his Father for the world, as is demonstrated in the *pro nobis,* the Christian is called to identification with him. From this follows the obligation to love God (and in God one's brothers and sisters) and to adore him in spirit and truth.

When Balthasar wrote the "Nine Theses" for the International Theological Commission, he had already completed the third volume

---

1. I refer to the famous "Nine Propositions on Christian Ethics," in *Principles of Christian Morality* (San Francisco, 1986), pp. 77-104; "A Word on 'Humanae Vitae,'" *New Elucidations,* pp. 204-28.

2. "Nine Propositions," pp. 79-84.

of the *Theo-Drama,* in which, crossing carefully over the rough waters of recent Catholic and Protestant exegesis, he endeavored to establish the absolute contemporaneity of the singular event of Christ to present human history, giving a careful reply to the unresolved Enlightenment objection, whose influence remains so pernicious for ethics even today: How can a contingent and historically situated fact serve as the foundation of universal and necessary truths?

On the basis of these two presuppositions Balthasar considers, respectively, natural law and Old Testament law as elements and fragments included in the concrete universal norm, namely, the event of Jesus Christ.[3]

Even at this level it is thus possible to include natural law in the Christ event and to oppose the unjustifiable notion of a heterogeneity between Christ and the natural law which would make the two factors totally incongruous. This assertion is the most pernicious of all those circulating today in the field of moral theology. On the one hand, it is responsible for the rejection of the natural law in the name of a reference to Christ that is so generic as to be incapable of founding the concrete moral norm; on the other, it accounts for the oblivion of the Christic foundation in the conviction that reference to the natural law alone is sufficient basis for the moral norm as such.

In this direction, Balthasar has shown how a *sequela Christi* rightly understood also resolves the problem of norms, provided that it has recourse to a correct systematic vision of the logic of salvation history.

What is the theological basis for such a statement? Concretely, it is found in an objectively Christocentric vision of man. This vision proceeds from the consideration of creative predestination in its relationship with natural law, on which depend both the foundations of morality and the solution to the *vexata quaestio* of the autonomy or heteronomy of a morality that is really suitable to the freedom of the person.[4] This vision reaches its term in the formulation of the correct relationship of the Christian's justification to his moral actions, and thereby founds the specifically Christian element in morality.

These are the essential terms for the theological study of the connection between anthropology and morality. Here, however, we will take into consideration only some general lines of reflection.

---

3. Ibid., pp. 89-104.
4. See the brilliant solution in ibid., pp. 80f.

The predestination of Jesus Christ and of every man to be a "son in the Son" is at the basis of Balthasar's Christocentrism. Predestination determines the existence of an essential solidarity of the entire human race in Christ. This solidarity explains the centrality of Christ, his headship, in the fullest sense, of humanity, and places Adam in a position of dependence with respect to Christ, the new Adam.[5] Such predestination is in reality definable in terms of a creative predestination.[6] In fact, theologically speaking, creation is nothing else than the effective fulfillment of predestination. Freedom, understood as the emblematic figure for all of anthropology, encounters at this level its own source and at the same time discovers its derived nature. Without losing its autonomy, freedom, in the Christocentric perspective, is included in grace.

The justification worked by Christ on the cross, however, finds freedom in a position of rupture with respect to grace, even though objectively freedom is included in grace from the beginning. In this case freedom is associated formally to the sin of Adam *(peccatum originale originans),* which is the foundation of a precise situation of guilt involving all of humanity *(peccatum originale originatum).*[7]

God the Father's saving plan, already enunciated in predestination, emerges in its full contours against the background of sin: his merciful initiative to forgive sins by *sending* his Son Jesus Christ, to which the decision of the Son to allow himself to be sent, even to the point of death on the cross, *propter nostram salutem,* corresponds in total obedience. The second formal datum emerging from sin is that man's liberty needs conversion in order to be able to receive the salvation merited by the dead and risen Christ. The whole business of anthropology, and so of ethics, thus appears marked by the interweaving of man's finite freedom and the infinite freedom of God.[8]

Examining the moral implications of this discussion more closely, we have to begin by advancing a premise. This concept of predestination and of justification rests on an adequate concept of anthropology. As we have already mentioned, the point here is a Christic

---

5. The theme recurs frequently in Balthasar. See, for example, *Theo-Drama,* III:33-40.

6. It is thus defined by Inos Biffi, "Integralità cristiana e fondazione morale," *La Scuola Cattolica* 115 (1987): 570-90.

7. "Nine Propositions," pp. 87-88.

8. Cf. *Theo-Drama,* vol. IV.

anthropology that asserts a single supernatural end of man.[9] This anthropology is able to conceive the logic of the history of salvation as distinct from its chronology.

This implies a kind of theological reflection within an integral perspective based on a whole in which, without confusion and without separation, nature and supernature, creation and redemption, essence and history all coexist. In fact, to speak of man's supernatural end, when it is understood as the sole, though gratuitous (it could also have been otherwise), end in the actual historical order,[10] inevitably leads us to conceive of creation as creation-elevation and of the creature, with its own constitutive metaphysical exigencies, within the covenant of salvation history. In the eyes of such an anthropology, ontology and history appear as inseparably joined from the beginning.[11]

This anthropology is opposed to the anthropology of the double end, for which nature is conceived as separate from the supernatural and, precisely in virtue of this separateness, is supposed to be capable of providing neutral ground on which to set universal and immutable contents. In this kind of perspective, creation establishes nature as a reality which stands more or less implicitly before redemption and is presupposed by it.[12] Nature is then conceived as the essence of man, while redemption is viewed as that reality which adds history to this essence. Consequently, nature offers the metaphysical, the immutable, and the universal, while redemption offers the historical, the mutable, and the contingent.[13] This is loaded with negative consequences for the way in which natural law is understood.

If after this clarification we return to the field of moral theology, we could say that creative predestination essentially coincides on the ethical plane with what the great theological tradition has dubbed "eternal law." Eternal law is the practical dimension of that great Trinitarian plan which is creative predestination.

We could without hesitation put it like this: since all laws, including the divine, are nothing other than the translation of Christic

---

9. *The Theology of Henri de Lubac,* pp. 61ff.; *The Theology of Karl Barth,* pp. 326-63.
10. DS, 2318.
11. *Theo-Drama,* III:250-59.
12. Cf. *The Christian State of Life.*
13. I. Biffi, "Integralità cristiana," pp. 582-83.

predestination, to which the eternal law objectively reduces, natural law, without any loss in its density, is no longer perceived as extrinsic in respect to the Christocentric perspective but is objectively included in it.[14] From this viewpoint the relationship between creation and redemption shows, in fact, how Christ, the new Adam, assumes all of the exigencies of the first Adam. The old law and natural law are thus objectively recapitulated in Christ; and the Christian, living in the last days, must not forget an elementary hermeneutical principle: The whole, which is in our case the coming of Christ, the concrete universal norm, becomes the regulating structure of all the fragmentary forms of ethics. We must not, therefore, reinterpret the *lex nova* in the light of old law or of the natural law. What is required is exactly the inverse process. Since man is included in Christ by means of justifying redemption, natural law is included in the divine law. But this redemptive inclusion is possible only if it represents the further determination of man's inclusion through predestination. Thus, in the final analysis the reduction of eternal law to predestination in Christ commands the entire system of laws.

This is a matter loaded with consequences that cannot be adequately explored here. It will suffice to cite briefly a principle and two facts. Inclusion is effected according to the model of the component or of the dialogue partner.[15] This signifies, first, that *ratio,* and thus natural law, continue to carry out their function within the whole, but without the erroneous distinction between essence (attributed to creation) and history (attributed to redemption). Second, the universal and necessary character belonging to natural law will appear to be objectively contained in the universality and immutability which are the prerogatives of Christic predestination.

Moreover, it should be noted that, even independently of this Christocentric perspective, Thomas asserts that the Decalogue and the natural law are assumed into the regime of the new law, while the ceremonial and judicial precepts of the Old Testament are allowed to lapse.[16] In full agreement with the perspective and principle alluded

14. This is the reason why Balthasar speaks of elements and of fragments in order to indicate the modality according to which old law and the natural law live in the concrete universal norm which is Jesus Christ. "Nine Propositions," pp. 89-102.

15. I. Biffi, "Integralità cristiana," pp. 584-85.

16. See A. Scola, *La fondazione teologica della legge naturale nello Scriptum super Sententiis di San Tommaso d'Aquino* (Freiburg, 1982), pp. 215-37.

to here, Saint Paul does not hesitate to affirm that even pagans will be judged "by means of Jesus Christ according to my gospel" (Rom. 2:16).

Such a christological and anthropological concentration of morality does not at all diminish the universality of ethics. On the contrary, it is precisely by being rooted in Christology, anthropology, and ecclesiology that ethics attains the note of a universality which is not purely formal. It now remains to overcome the false conviction that only a natural ethic can be universal and the resulting conclusion, as pernicious as it is illogical, that the Christocentric reference constrains ethics to become regionalized, causing it to lose universality. We are all familiar with the resultant impasse in which ethics is kept today even by many Christian thinkers (and not just ethics, since the same reasoning is applied to social doctrine): an ethics which appeals openly to faith is regional and by nature nonuniversal, while thinking in terms of natural law is fallacious, therefore . . . in ethics there are no universally valid absolute norms. I think it is possible to avoid the notion that thinking in terms of natural law is in itself fallacious; but it is certainly possible adequately to found essential and universal ethical norms on the basis of the Christocentric vision of reality.

Nor is it valid to object, "How then will we be able to speak to those who do not believe? In the name of what can there be an understanding with them?" Such an objection forgets that natural law is assumed in Christ and in the new law. And that which is assumed is not abolished: *quod est assumptum est servatum.* It is always possible to show the nonbeliever the intrinsic reasonableness of a norm which can also be known naturally, without a priori waiving the right to present it as an ingredient of a whole whose full foundation is given only in the perspective of Christ.

On this basis one understands why for Balthasar "existence in Christ," besides identifying the theological person, that is, his mission, is a fact that touches him in his most intimate self, ontologically transforming him. Balthasar's concept of the Christian mission is not that of an assignment which man can decide and carry forward by virtue of his ethical capacities. It is entirely received by grace from above and holds an all-consuming grip on man, even on contemporary man. For Balthasar Christian morality is inconceivable except as the perfected realization of all that is human, if not as the sole reasonable chance offered to the man of today. Thus, for Balthasar there is no *sequela Christi* that does not explicitly bear witness. One need think only of the coincidence of person and mission in Christ, on which the acute christological sketch of the *Theo-Drama* rests.

If the mission makes the person, we cannot see how the Christian, formed by his belonging to Christ, can conceive his morality other than as a being taken into service by the Church for the world.[17]

17. *The Heart of the World* (San Francisco, 1980).

CHAPTER TEN

"A House Full of
Open Doors . . ."

"God is not a sealed fortress, to be attacked and seized by our engines of war (ascetic practices, meditative techniques, and the like), but a house full of open doors, through which we are invited to walk. In the Castle of the Three-in-One, the plan has always been that we, those who are entirely 'other,' shall participate in the super-abundant communion of life."[1]

The *form* of Balthasar's theology could find in this passage from one of his homilies on the Trinity a crystal on which to reflect all its light.

First of all there is the Trinitarian "being-with" of the "Three-in-One," in which the one Being of God continually gives and receives itself in the loving exchange between the Persons. It is this original love, well expressed by the term "with," from which everything comes and to which everything returns.

From it comes creation, as an additional gift which the Father makes to the Son, the Son makes to the Father, and the Spirit makes to both; because precisely in virtue of the actions of each of the Persons the world, from the moment of creation, participates in God and, at the end, renders to him what it has received of the divine.

The destiny of divine sonship to which man (though endowed with his own nature and freedom) is called from all time is not shattered even when man opposes God with his pretense to *autosoteria* and sinks into the alienation of sin.

1. *You Crown the Year with Your Goodness,* p. 188.

How will the sinner ever be able to find by himself the road back to that destiny of exhilarating communion, opened up to him out of pure grace by the Trinitarian "with"? He would find it impossible; but behold — sublimity of God's omnipotence — once again the embrace of the Trinitarian "with" surprises him from below, from the depths of his separation. The omnipotence of him who is love in no way fears the *kenosis* of the cross. And the Son — pure, holy, and immaculate victim — allows himself to be sacrificed in our place, *pro nobis,* obedient to the will of the Father, which the Spirit, as unifier, places before him even in the moment of the transfixed cry of supreme abandonment. The *apostolos,* he who is sent, traverses the abyss of malediction and sin to its extreme limits. He, who knew not sin and was even carried in the virginal womb and accompanied by the "awakening Thou" of Mary Immaculate, allows himself to be disposed of at the *hour* of the *consummation.*

Because of this mission of obedience, history takes a turn in the sepulchre of Christ: every instant of its time passes into the form of Christ's uique and unrepeatable death. And when the Father's Love flings away the stone covering the sepulchre, the glory of Christ gives the whole of humanity a renewed and full access to the constitutive *form,* the *Gloria Dei,* which from all time had been included in the mysterious beauty of being and of every entity, but which only "in Christ," the complete form, is unveiled according to that design surpassing the comprehension of every human mind in which merciful love is disclosed for the life of men.

The Spirit poured forth by the Crucified opens the way to follow Christ and convokes the Church from everywhere as the new setting for the life of the redeemed. In her they will find their own specific mission and consequently their unrepeatable personality. The Church as the living presence of his glory, the *signum elevatum in nationibus,* will not cease to fascinate man.

Christ's claim is placed once and for all at the heart of history, and every man will have to make his reckoning with the Nazarene. His is an unarmed power: the power of the cross, of the Eucharist in which he, everywhere on earth and in all ages, is perpetually given. To whom? To our freedom with its obstinate capacity for rejection, rejection that takes a thousand forms, characterized above all by a forgetfulness that knows no limits.

Christ is indeed life's "serious case"; but will men want to realize this? At bottom, the destiny of every human existence is contained in this question.

However much the name of Christ may seem insignificant in the life of contemporary men, however much they exist in solitary preoccupation with their problems and interests, however much Christians themselves or even men of the Church may have lost sight of the fresh living water of his presence, the miracle of the encounter, which is pure grace, repeats itself. No one can remove it from history. Now as then, in the mystery of the encounter with one who, though unworthy, has been seized by the beauty of his form, his invitation can resound in the hearts of men of every race: "Zacchaeus, come down. I am going to your house." And the miracle of change takes place: a mission stands before life and a new personality takes shape.

Christ's form, then, lives wherever two or three are gathered in his name, moved by the charisms which his Spirit unceasingly causes to flower, like new buds on the old and living trunk of his Church.

And so it will be until the end, when the "house full of open doors" will be filled by the presence of the saved.

And what about the tragedy of those who can refuse the "underembrace" of the Trinity to the last? This question engaged Balthasar in close debate to the final days of his life. His position on the subject was grossly distorted, and he was not spared the bitterness of grave and offensive misunderstandings. He never stated that hell does not exist nor that it is empty; he wanted merely to safeguard the datum of New Testament revelation which authorizes us to *hope for all* people.

Might not *hope* be the last word of such a dizzying theological form? Especially when it attempts to penetrate the crucified glory of our Lord and the participation of the Triune God in the drama of Golgotha and, through it, in that of every man of all ages?

Surprised by John Paul II's decision to name him Cardinal, Balthasar acquiesced, not without qualms, with the obedience of one who has been "taken into service." He found support in his great love for the Pope and for Cardinal Ratzinger, his devoted friend. One evening during Balthasar's final days on earth, he remarked to a few friends who, having overcome his natural shyness, were holding a little party in his honor, "If you, my friends, are happy, then I must be happy too." He said this without design and without affectation. I was struck by the extraordinary simplicity of faith in a man endowed with such a vast and astute intelligence and a heart capable of receiving and mitigating the most searing anguish.

Is this perhaps the secret of his depth? The *form* of the glorious Lord shines most brightly on the countenance of the simple.